# The Successful Career Toolkit

Your quick-fire guide to mastering business skills

Patrick Barr

KoganPage

First published in Great Britain and the United States in 2019 by Kogan Page Limited

2nd Floor, 45 Gee Street
London
EC1V 3RS
United Kingdom
www.koganpage.com

122 W 27th St, 10th Floor
New York, NY 10001
USA

4737/23 Ansari Road
Daryaganj
New Delhi 110002
India

**ISBNs**

Hardback    978 0 7494 9876 4
Paperback   978 0 7494 8477 4
Ebook       978 0 7494 8478 1

**British Library Cataloguing-in-Publication Data**

A CIP record for this book is available from the British Library.

**Library of Congress Cataloging-in-Publication Data**
Names: Barr, Patrick, author.
Title: The successful career toolkit : your quick-fire guide to mastering
    business skills / Patrick Barr.
Description: 1 Edition. | New York : Kogan Page Ltd, [2019] | Includes index.
Identifiers: LCCN 2018058325| ISBN 9780749484774 (pbk.) | ISBN 9780749498764
    (hardback) | ISBN 9780749484781 (ebook)
Subjects: LCSH: Career development. | Vocational guidance. | Success in
    business.
Classification: LCC HF5381 .B3187 2019 | DDC 650.1–dc23 LC record available at
    https://lccn.loc.gov/2018058325

Typeset by Integra Software Services, Pondicherry
Print production managed by Jellyfish
Printed and bound by CPI Group (UK) Ltd, Croydon CR0 4YY

*To Sheila, Niall and James, family and friends who have inspired and supported me always!*

# CONTENTS

# ABOUT THE AUTHOR

Patrick Barr has over 20 years' international leadership experience in operations, supply chain and strategic management. He has held senior roles in Ireland, the UK and the USA in the airline, FMCG and IT industry sectors. He is currently the owner and Managing Partner of Barr Performance Coaching. His clients are predominantly senior leaders in both domestic and international enterprises ranging in scale from micro SMEs to major multinationals. Prior to taking on his current role, Patrick was a senior director at Microsoft with responsibility for leading a major operating model change programme. Previously at Microsoft he had responsibility for leading the global OEM physical and digital supply chain team. Prior to joining Microsoft Patrick attained an MBA from University College Dublin and held senior supply chain and procurement management positions at Diageo and British Airways. He is passionate about leadership development and performance management and has attained postgraduate qualifications in business mentoring and leadership coaching. He is a member of the Enterprise Ireland Mentor Panel, a faculty member of the Irish Management Institute, a member of the European Mentoring & Coaching Council and the International Coach Federation, and joined the board of the ISPCC in July 2016. He is a qualified Hogan Psychometric Assessment practitioner. Patrick is married with two sons and lives in Dublin.

# ACKNOWLEDGEMENTS

I would like to thank the team in Kogan Page for having the confidence to pursue the project through to publication and in particular Rebecca Bush for her thoughtful, patient guidance through the editing process. During the course of writing this book many people were very generous in giving of their time and expertise in providing insightful, practical and inspiring feedback. I would especially like to thank the following for their encouragement, support and sharing of their invaluable perspectives.

Robert Barr
Kevin Blair
Ciaran Boyle
Colette Cahalane
Hannah Carney
Paul Delahunty
June Duffy
Todd Dunlap
Marcella Flood
Dr. Colm Foster
Brian Gilsenan
Tom Jordan
David Lane

Emily Manning
Dermot McMahon
Eamonn O'Casarlaigh
Orla O'Connor
Michael O'Donovan
Ray O'Neill
Stephanie Peterson
Mike Quinn
Julie Ralston
Mark Saunders
Andre Severi
Una Tynan
David Warrick

# HOW TO USE THIS BOOK

In order to equip yourself with the essential skills you will need throughout your career I suggest you keep this compendium of quick-fire practical solutions close and use it as a reference guide, prior to taking action. There are topics to support you throughout your career – from learning how to manage yourself, to thinking about managing tasks and processes, and on to managing and leading others – and whether you want to learn the essentials of each situation, or refresh the knowledge you already have, this toolkit is designed to provide you with quick and easy-to-apply guidance.

You can certainly read it from cover to cover if you are so inclined, but what I would suggest for best results is to read the chapter relevant to the particular work situation you're facing, reflect upon the content and then do the exercise at the end so that you can practise putting it into action. If you have a trusted confidant, mentor or coach, each chapter should provide you with food for thought, so that you can make the most of your engagement with those individuals. Leadership and business decision-making are rarely 'solo runs': the more people you can engage in the discussion, the better the likelihood of a more rewarding outcome.

Ultimately, I would like you to be inspired to be your best self and reach whatever level of fulfilment you desire – this book is intended to provide you with the tools that you need to do so.

# PART ONE
# Managing self

# 01
# Communication skills

Good, well-structured communication should inspire an audience to actively support you in your endeavours. High-quality communication can help inspire trust in you, it can defuse potentially stressful situations and reduce anxiety in your audience by removing ambiguity. The opposite is also true: a badly written or presented topic can provoke a reaction in the audience that can result in loss of faith. Honing your communication skills is a critical aspect of continuous professional development.

## Written communication

The points below are generally true for emails, newsletters, formal communications and white papers.

> Tip: communication is not about sharing information or data; it is about giving *meaning* to the information and the data.

### Before you start

- **Audience:** Who is your audience? What preconceptions or hopes and fears do they bring to the topic? Why should they care about your message? Do they have a good understanding of the context and background to your communication? How do they like to receive content?
- **Purpose:** Why are you sending this communication and why are you sending it now? Is it a briefing document, an update or a message that you are hoping will elicit action or change?

- **Desired outcome:** Are you clear on what response or action you are hoping to elicit from the person who reads the email or document? Be very clear, make the reader aware of your expectations early in the content.

In most business communications, less is more – be brief and to the point.

## Communication structure

- **Title:** the title must evoke an interest in the reader and inspire them to read the content.
- **Introduction:** a concise summary of why the content is important to the reader, (why now?) and expectations of next steps.
- **Context:** provide information that helps the reader orient to the context and level of urgency of the topic.
- **Definition of the issue or key opportunity:** this needs to be concise, factual and supported by data; it should clearly outline the scope of the topic.
- **Impact:** describe the impact in terms of measurable/quantifiable outcomes as they pertain to customer, competition, costs, revenue, people or risk to brand reputation.
- **Help wanted:** describe any specific help wanted from the audience.
- **Next steps:** outline short- and long-term next steps, clearly stating the following:
  - What action will be taken?
  - Who is responsible for taking the action?
  - When will the action happen?
  - What outcome is expected?
  - Summarize for the audience what they can expect to see or hear over the next few weeks, focusing specifically on communications and the plan for updates.

# Due diligence

- **Sense check:** once you have put the content into writing, it can take on a life of its own. Would you be happy for the content of the communication to appear – out of context – with your name attached, on the internet or the front page of a newspaper? How would a third party view you as a result of reading the email/document?

- **Length:** in the modern world if you have not captured the attention of the reader within the first few sentences the probability is that they will stop reading and move on to something else. If you find your content extending to more than one page, you probably need to put in an executive summary. Remember, in most communications, less is more!

- **Language:** Are you using language that will resonate with the audience? Check that you have not been overly technical or used words/phrases that can be open to multiple interpretations. Have you used acronyms that the audience will understand? Will the language you use evoke the desired outcome from the reader? Make the message relevant to the audience: really good communicators are able to make the topic real by explaining it in a manner that is engaging to the reader.

- **Facts and data:** facts and data generate perspectives – don't assume everyone is drawing the same conclusions from the data. Be sure to circle back with the audience to check on their perspective by asking for feedback on your conclusions.

- **Pause:** if you are writing about a topic for which you have a great passion or if you are writing an email about an emotional topic it is probably a good idea to pause before hitting the send button. In business communication it is OK to challenge and disagree with content or another person's point of view, but the challenge or disagreement should never be capable of being perceived as a personal attack on the other person. If necessary, get a third party to read the content before sending.

- **Email delay:** it is possible to change the setting on your email so that there is a delay between you hitting the send button and the email actually leaving your outbox. Some people will deliberately set a 10- or 15-minute delay in their email settings; this gives them time to stop an email going out even after they have hit the send button.

# Presentations

The rules of good communication are generally consistent across media – specifically, clarity of purpose and relevance to the audience being the most important. However, there are some aspects that are particularly important for presentations.

## *Storytelling*

Remember to be brief and to the point. However, in a verbal presentation you need to tell a story or bring your points to life in a manner that will resonate with the audience. It can be helpful to illustrate your points with real-life scenarios and show the impact of your proposed actions. A well-told story that catches the imagination of the audience will have a much greater impact than simply laying out the facts. The key to success is to ensure that the core theme and message of the story aligns with the key points that you want to make. If there is a disconnect between the story and your key points, then it is likely the audience will be confused – so choose your story carefully.

Key questions that your presentation should answer:

● Why are you passionate about this topic?

● Why should the audience care, and why should they care now?

● What do the audience truly need to know for them to be successful?

● What will the audience learn from listening to you?

## *Presentation structure*

Note that slides should not be designed to be read; they should simply be bullet points designed to evoke curiosity or be a placeholder for the topic. Too much slide content will distract from what you are saying – less is more!

● **Slide 1 – intro and agenda:** introduce yourself, outline the purpose or objective of the presentation and what you will cover during the presentation. At this point you need to acknowledge the audience, especially if there are imbalances of familiarity with the topic, ie the audience includes some subject matter experts and some people who are completely new to the topic. If you have an audience with differing levels of subject knowledge, you will need to take some time to bring everyone up to a base level of knowledge. At the end of Slide 1, stop and sense check with the audience that your interpretation of their interest in/needs from the presentation is accurate.

● **Slide 2 – context:** describe the business challenge. It may be good to use a story or scenario to illustrate how the topic is relevant in the real world. Provide information that gives background to help the audience orient to the scale and level of urgency of the topic.

- **Slide 3 – define the issue or key opportunity:** this needs to be concise, factual and supported by data, and it should clearly outline the scope of the topic. In the context of an issue, you should outline the root cause and/or facts that back up your hypothesis.

- **Slide 4 – solution:** describe the solution or path forward for the future, ie what will be different and how will you measure success? Describe the impact in terms of material measurable/quantifiable outcomes as they pertain to customer, competition, costs, revenue, people or risk to brand reputation.

- **Slide 5 – summary and actions:** summarize the learning or what the audience should take away from your presentation. Include next steps, where you outline short- and long-term next steps, clearly stating the following:

  - What action will be taken?
  - Who is responsible for taking the action?
  - When will the action happen?
  - What outcome is expected?
  - Summarize for the audience what they can expect to see or hear over the next few weeks, focusing specifically on communications and the plan for updates.
  - Include your contact details and an offer to help those who would like to know more.

## Sense check

Having written the slides it is important to sense check that what you have written will resonate with the audience. Put yourself in the position of the audience – are you delivering the content in a manner that is empathetic to the audience needs? How will a third party view you as a result of attending the presentation?

Are you using language that will resonate with the audience? Check that you have not been overly technical or used words and phrases that can be open to multiple interpretations. Have you used acronyms that the audience will not understand? Will the language you use evoke the desired outcome from the audience? Avoid analogies – you may think you are conveying something clearly, but the audience may be getting a totally different understanding. This is especially true if the audience is culturally diverse.

The slide content should support your presentation and not distract from your verbal message. If the audience is reading your slide, they are probably not listening. Remember, the slide should not be simply another version of your verbal content – and you should *never* read from the slide!

## Presentation delivery

Much of what you say in your presentation is reinforced by *how* you present the content. Your body language, tone and physical presence make a difference to your overall impact. Show your passion for the topic! Your audience will respond positively to your energy and interest in the topic. Don't forget to smile and make eye contact with the audience. It is a good idea to stand when you are presenting to ensure that you are visible; don't hide behind a lectern. Present in a clear, even and conversational tone. Where possible arrive in good time and check out the venue: what will be your route onto the stage? What type of microphone will be used? Will sunlight blind the audience? Are there external noises you need to account for?

Wear comfortable clothing that will camouflage, or at the very least not accentuate, the by-product of nerves, eg if you are prone to sweating when nervous, wear loose fitting clothes. If your hands or brow are prone to sweating, try to carry a tissue in your pocket. Wear clothing that will keep you warm, as you don't want to be shivering with the cold as well as nerves. Do your best to prepare, reduce stress levels and thereby minimize the risks with a few key reminders:

- Prepare prompt cards with key words to help you through your presentation – you may not use them, but the activity of writing the cards will help you think through your presentation in a slow and methodical manner. Knowing that you have the cards as backup will also give you confidence.

- Don't wear jewellery that will make a noise, rattle or distract as you move around.

- Don't bring non-essential items to the meeting.

- Reduce your caffeine intake prior to the meeting.

- Where possible, arrive in good time and check out the physical surroundings to prevent any surprises.

Aim to capture the audience's attention within the first few minutes of your presentation, and check in with the audience to see that you are meeting their needs. You should always have three versions of your presentation: a micro version (3 minutes), a standard version (10 minutes), and a long version (30 minutes), which allows you to accelerate or slow your presentation depending on audience needs. The rule of thumb: **10-20-30** may help:

- No more than **10** slides.
- No more than **20** minutes.
- Font size no smaller than **30**-point.

Remember, in a presentation you never know what you have communicated until you see the audience react. Don't assume that the audience understood your points in the way you intended; they will bring their own perspective to the presentation that may distort their understanding of your content. To validate the understanding, always allow time for questions from the audience to you, and from you to the audience.

It is important to be yourself – be genuine and honest, and if you don't believe in what you're presenting, don't present it. If you don't know an answer to a question, ask if you can take it away and respond at a later date, rather than try to bluff an answer in the moment. If you need more time to think of an answer to a question, you can always ask the person to give you more context to their question. This buys you a little time to formulate your answer.

Speak slowly: the probability is that the audience have turned up because they want to hear what you have to say – so don't rush it. Take deep breaths and go slowly.

# Dealing with apprehension and nerves

The first thing to remember is that nerves occur naturally and are a good thing! Nerves are the physiological manifestation of heightened awareness, driven by a belief that we need to be more alert to our surroundings. Before any major presentation or important meeting, we *should* be a little nervous – nerves are simply nature's way of preparing us to enter a situation of uncertainty or exit from our comfort zone.

In summary, nerves are good!

- Nerves are nature's way of raising our awareness of our surroundings.
- Nerves sharpen your senses.

- Nerves remind you of the importance of the occasion.
- Nerves show to the audience you care.
- Nerves suppress other distractions that are not relevant to the situation.

The best way to deal with nerves is to acknowledge them, ie tell people you are nervous. It is perfectly OK to open a meeting or presentation by saying 'I am a bit nervous because you are a very key audience/customer/stakeholder and it is important to me that this meeting/presentation goes well'. By acknowledging the nerves you are being authentic and honest – two attributes most audiences will find endearing.

Nerves tend to become negative or destructive when we try to hide them or deny them.

---

### Tips, tricks and takeaways

- **Recognition:** if the content is not your own, remember to give credit or due recognition to the creator or source of the content.
- **Solicit feedback:** try to work feedback into your communication process. Whether it is a written document or a presentation, any feedback you can get in advance will help you deliver a better-quality message. All of the best writers and presenters in the world make use of editors and other skilled professionals to hone their content before they publish or present – you should be no different!
- **Slide transitions:** moving from one slide to the next can sometimes be a trigger for interruptions, as some audience members don't want you to leave the slide until they have asked a question. It can be good to solicit a question from the audience before moving to the next slide, eg 'Is everyone OK if I move on to the next slide?'
- **Practice makes perfect!** This is very true for presentations. If you can, do a dry run with someone; if not, present to yourself in front of a mirror or try to record yourself so that you can check how you sound – avoid repeating pet phrases or sound bites. Specifically: time yourself. A presentation should proceed at a measured pace – it is not a race to the end.
- **Try to avoid platitudes:** for example, responding to a question with 'That's a great question...'. While it's fine to acknowledge a good question, don't start every answer in the same way.

## Reflective exercise

Record yourself. It is good to hear yourself speak. Play back the recording and ask yourself how you would respond if you heard the presentation. If your communication is written, it may be useful to record yourself reading the document aloud and then play it back to yourself, to see if the language resonates with you.

# 02
# My curriculum vitae

The CV (or résumé) is the document that you hope will differentiate you from the competition in the eyes of a potential employer. It is your own personal marketing document – your brand – it represents you when you are not in the room. A strong CV will help you stand out from the crowd and will include all of the items below to a greater or lesser extent.

There are plenty of CV formats to choose in Microsoft Word or from elsewhere on the internet. Choose one that you feel will help you get your key points across. Sharp clean lines with no clutter work best. (See two format samples in Appendices 1 and 2 on pages 201 and 202.)

## What should I include in my CV?

### Focus on your achievements

For a hiring manager, it is not what you have done but what you have delivered that is important. In order to stand out, talk about achievements and deliverables, as opposed to inputs. Many people make the mistake of highlighting simply what they did instead of what the outcome was in their work experience to date. What impact have you had in your current and previous roles? You will be hired for what you are capable of delivering, not just working hard. Your deliverables should be factual, measurable and clearly attributable to you.

Focus on impact! In other words, *what* you delivered and *how* you delivered it. Business impact is usually summarized in the following areas:

- **Revenue or sales increases:** activities or innovations that drove a material increase in revenue. Remember, the outcome should be quantifiable.

  Example: I implemented a new sales strategy that drove an $x$ per cent year-on-year sales increase; or I led a new marketing initiative that drove a $y$ per cent increase in market share.

- **Cost reduction:** improvement that reduced cost or improved efficiency.

  Example: I drove an operating process review that resulted in a $y$ per cent reduction in cost per unit year on year.

- **Customer satisfaction:** any activities or initiatives that improved customer retention and by extension improved sales or at the very least improved the likelihood of the customer recommending your company or brand to a friend.

  Example: I worked as part of a team to implement a process change that resolved a specific customer pain point, which resulted in an $x$ per cent increase in customer satisfaction and increased the likelihood of the customer making a repeat purchase.

- **Team performance/management/leadership:** What do you do that improves team morale or inspires others to raise their game? What do you do to develop others?

  Example: I initiated a mentoring programme; or I acted as a coach; or I improved team morale scores through the introduction of a new feedback programme.

- **Strategy:** What do you do that secures the future?

  Example: I recognized the requirement to periodically take the team out of the day-to-day to focus on longer-term challenges and opportunities, which resulted in less firefighting and energized the team as they felt ownership for the strategy and securing future company success.

- **Minimize risk:** What did you do to eliminate or reduce risk in the process or improve compliance?

  Example: I ensured that we undertook a comprehensive due diligence exercise on an annual basis, to identify and mitigate all key risks and stress-test all critical processes.

It is not critical to have an impact in *all* of the above areas, but the more senior the role you are applying for, the more areas you will be expected to cover.

## *Be succinct, relevant and impactful*

Less is more – the person reading your CV is looking for facts that are critically relevant to the role. Tailor your CV to the job description of the role for which you are applying. Remember your CV may be read by a machine or an individual who has no knowledge of the position that is being hired, and so they will be looking out for key words. These key words will usually be found in the job description. Go through the job description and pick out the key competencies and experience that the role requires, and ensure that you have highlighted those features in your CV.

## Continuous professional development

Most employers will look for a commitment to continuous professional development. Education is not something that stops when you leave school or university. It is good to show that you are passionate about learning and developing yourself further. All qualifications should be listed.

## Soft skills

The vast majority of roles involve working closely with colleagues or clients, and in many cases this may involve cultural sensitivities and respect for diversity. Where possible, illustrate that you have the skills and competencies to work positively with all types of people and that you will respect diverse views and customs.

## Balance

An employer probably doesn't want to hire a robot; they will be looking for someone who will contribute to the team and the culture of the business. It is important to show that you have balance in your life and that you actively contribute to helping others by serving on committees or another voluntary activity within a charity, club or organization. It is important that there is a connection between what you share as interests and hobbies and the competencies highlighted in the job description or the organization's values. Remember – if this information won't show how you will succeed in the role and at the company, there is no need to include it.

## Personal profile

Many people include a 50–80-word personal profile at the beginning of their CV – it is, in essence, an executive summary of your CV or a written version of your elevator pitch. If you are including one you must make it enticing and impactful, otherwise the reader will not read the rest of your CV. It must be relevant to the job and highlight what makes you uniquely suited to the role.

# Structuring your CV

When it comes to compiling your CV, this is a typical structure to follow:

**1** Personal details (address, email and contact number).

**2** Personal profile (optional).

**3** List of your skills and achievements (optional).

**4** Your work experience. Start with the most recent role and work back, focusing on what you delivered and what impact you had, rather than just describing your work. Focus on what is relevant to the role you are applying for.

**5** Education and training qualifications.

**6** Hobbies and interests (optional; but don't underestimate the importance of balance).

**7** References on request. There is no need to list referees at this point, unless specifically requested.

# What is the two-page rule?

There is a general 'two-page rule' for a CV, even if you have substantial experience that looks like it will need more than two pages. Challenge yourself to be concise. Be sure to question whether each piece of information is going to help get you an interview – if it isn't, then there is no need to include it.

Remember, being able to communicate in a succinct and impactful way is probably a competency you want to demonstrate, thus less is more.

Despite the concise nature of a two-page CV, it is important to remember that the first page is absolutely critical – you need to 'hook' the reader early in the document.

## Tips, tricks and takeaways

- **LinkedIn:** make sure your LinkedIn profile is consistent with what you have put on your CV. A recruiter may well cross-reference your CV with your LinkedIn profile.

- **Should I add a picture?** Some companies may ask for a picture, but most will at least look at your LinkedIn profile (and possibly your Facebook profile and other social media) so make sure the picture is a suitable, professional photo. As an aside, LinkedIn profiles with pictures are 14 times more likely to be looked at than those with no picture (Hulse, 2018). A picture of you playing with your kids or in holiday mode may show your playful side, but is probably not ideal for a professional purpose.

- **Style:** CVs will vary in style and layout; however, your CV should always be easy to read and convey what is relevant to the role for which you are applying.

- **Spelling and grammar:** if at all possible, get a third party to proofread your CV. Ideally, they will look out for poor punctuation, overuse of certain words, inappropriate use of acronyms and appropriate grammar. Remember, even commonly used acronyms may have different meanings in different industries.

- **Accuracy:** never lie in your CV! Your integrity is paramount; once you compromise your integrity you run the risk of doing untold damage to your career. Stick to the relevant facts. If an employer discovers a factual error or lie in your CV they can withdraw an offer – or if you have already joined the company, they can terminate your employment with immediate effect.

- **Humour:** humour can be subject to interpretation, personal taste or even mood of the person reading your CV. You cannot determine how humour will land, so it is best to avoid it in a CV.

- **Referees:** make sure your chosen referees are aware that they may receive a call, and are aware of what you have put in your CV and what you told the prospective employer in your interviews. A referee can give you a very positive reference but unwittingly undermine your chances of a job offer by giving a different perspective of events.

- **Follow up:** if you have submitted a CV for a role and had no response, it is reasonable to make contact with the company HR representative or hiring manager to check that your CV was received.

## Reflective exercise

1   Write down the top four or five proudest moments or achievements of your career.

2   Who benefited and how did they benefit from the moments listed in question 1 above?

3   What skills and competencies did you use to achieve your proudest moments?

Now check: are these highlights included in your CV? You may choose not to include them in the CV; however, you may like to use this content to form the basis of your answers to potential interview questions. The benefit of including this content in your CV is that it may give rise to questions in the interview, and you are more likely to talk enthusiastically, confidently and passionately about your proudest moments than any other topic.

# Reference

Hulse, T (2018) Opportunity knocks, *British Airways Business Life*, May, p. 45

# 03
# Career planning

Did you know that the majority of the qualities required to be successful are attitude based? Therefore, success is within your control.

Your working life will probably span a number of decades, so it wouldn't be unusual to have a number of different careers over the years. An individual may work in one profession, discipline or industry for 20 years and then decide to reinvent themselves and do something completely different. Career planning is an ongoing process.

## What are the 4Ps?

The ability to 'reinvent' yourself is becoming increasingly important, and successful people tend to operate to a simple model known as the 4Ps – purpose, perseverance, passion, and plan.

### Purpose

It is important to take the time out to assess what it is that will bring you long-term fulfilment in life. What is going to make you feel proud of your life? Your career may or may not be an integral part of your life's work; after all, some people 'live to work' and some people 'work to live'. It is important to understand where your career fits in the context of your life. Your purpose becomes an integral part of who you are.

To help with the process, you can imagine that you are writing your own obituary – not for any maudlin purpose, but to help you imagine what you would like your life's story to be. What went well? What disappointed you? When did you feel most fulfilled? What have you learnt about yourself along the way? It is very important to spend time really understanding what it is you want and *why* you want it.

## Perseverance

Focused people understand that to achieve a goal, sacrifices may have to be made along the way. Ultimately, there will almost certainly be trade-offs as you prioritize your next steps. You need to be willing to continue in the face of this adversity, and recognize that if something is worth having it will require hard work and ingenuity to achieve.

Fundamentally, you should expect to have setbacks and be predisposed to viewing them as learning opportunities, rather than roadblocks.

## Passion

Your life's goals should become a source of positive energy. The journey in itself will be rewarding and give you a sense of wellbeing and satisfaction. You should be passionate about your life's purpose, and express that excitement as appropriate. Being able to effectively communicate this passion will inspire others to help you achieve your purpose.

## Plan

Life becomes random if there is no plan; certainly, the probability of achieving a goal diminishes considerably if there is not a written plan. It is critical to share your plan, so that others can get an understanding of how they can support you.

Many people make the mistake of keeping their plan in their heads. However, keeping your thoughts in your head means they are likely to remain a dream, as opposed to the foundation for a successful outcome. Ultimately the quality of your plan determines your likelihood of success. It is important to note that the probability of successfully executing your plan can be greatly enhanced if three specific actions are taken:

1 Write down the plan.
2 Share your plan with a third party.
3 Set dates to review progress with the third party.

A plan is a road map that is put in place at a point in time; it should be flexible enough to allow you to respond to opportunities that will arise. It forms the basis from which you will make considered changes. A plan can and should change over time; it is not meant to be a straitjacket, or limit you in any way. It is there to enhance the probability of you achieving your career goal.

# Career planning process

**Take stock:** take time out to determine your life goals and how your career can help you in achieving fulfilment as you strive to attain them. At this point, it is important to take a long-term perspective, and think about your values as well as what will truly be best for you. Be careful of self-limiting beliefs – these are possibly unfounded assumptions that restrict your ambition. We sometimes kill an aspiration before we start by thinking too conservatively about what we are capable of in the long term. Essentially, you want to answer the following questions:

- What is important to me in life? What are my priorities? If I had no restrictions, what would I do? If I was not afraid, what would I do?
- What assets (skills, experience and competencies) do I have? Why would anyone want to be led by me? What is my 'brand'?
- What do I need to learn?

**Explore:** review what options are out there for you as you try to achieve your life goals. The questions below may be helpful:

- Am I looking for a vocation or a career or both?
- What type of role might I be best suited to?
- Do I want to work in the public or private sector?
- Do I want to work for a major multinational or a small indigenous company?
- Am I looking to work in a fast-paced, high-change environment or a more deliberate slow-paced environment?

**Sense check:** work with a trusted adviser to review your assumptions and answers to the questions in the sections above. The discipline of having to explain your logic and approach to a third party may prompt more ideas and will help you crystallize your thoughts. Hearing yourself explain your reasoning is also a useful exercise.

**Execute and review:** having done the above research, now is the time to write out a plan. Identify actions to improve your skills, competencies and experience; ensure that you are taking actions to keep your strengths current and to meaningfully address development areas. Be very specific on actions you will take to advance your career. It is generally good to always have a 'Plan B', as a good career plan will include more than one route to attain the ultimate goal.

**Solicit allies:** a key part of career management is to ensure that you have a network that is aware of your career aspirations and is prepared to support you on your journey. Set up a series of meetings with key allies to ensure that your relationship remains strong and that they know what you would like from them. The old adage, 'out of sight, out of mind' is very true – you need to keep your allies well briefed on your achievements, what you want to do next, and where you are looking to get to in the long term.

**Exposure:** many people assume the quality of their work will get them noticed. Unfortunately, it is often not that simple. The more senior you are, the more important (and frankly, necessary) it is to manage your profile and to promote yourself.

The bottom line is that the individual making a recruitment decision is taking a risk – the perceived risk is reduced if the hiring manager feels they know or have heard of the candidate. People rarely recruit complete strangers to senior roles; usually there has been some sort of networking or facilitated introduction that creates a connection, or you have a strong public profile. If you are not actively managing your exposure, that critical connection to the hiring manager may be lost. Certainly, the hiring manager will never come looking to headhunt someone they have never heard of. You can read more in Chapter 11 on managing your personal brand and Chapter 12 on effective networking.

## Tips, tricks and takeaways

- **Your plan:** look upon your plan as your 'road map' to success. It is not a straitjacket – you can always deviate from and revise the plan, but at least you do so from a recognized starting point with a clear set of assumptions. That way, you are making a considered change, as opposed to reacting to life's ups and downs in a haphazard manner. A plan that is in your head is not a plan, it is a dream!

- **Next role +1 – springboards and gateways:** it is good to think about what your next role will lead to – will the role you are targeting act as a springboard or gateway to other opportunities? What skills, competencies and experience will you acquire or enhance as a result of taking the role? Always ask yourself – will the role you are considering increase the probability of you reaching your long-term goal?

- **Career preference tests:** there are free online career preference tests that you can take, which may help you narrow down your search for the next type of role simply by eliminating those careers that you know do not appeal to you.

- **Being good at something:** don't fall into the 'You would be good at that' trap. Many people are very good at taking on roles that give them no satisfaction or sense of long-term fulfilment. They fall into such roles because they are seduced by the praise and possibly remuneration they receive for being good at the role; just because you are good at something does not mean it will give you long-term satisfaction. It is always better to focus on a balance of what you enjoy as well as what you are good at.

- **Grades:** don't let high academic grades distort your thinking. Some people feel that because they have high academic grades they should go on to university or pursue a career that requires high grades. Some people end up in careers because they had the qualifications, rather than truly wanting to pursue the career. Take the time to really understand what will make you feel fulfilled in the long run.

- **Select a career confidant:** this individual should be someone who knows you well, but can also be objective – probably not a partner or family member – who will help you orient your thoughts and hold you accountable for delivering the actions on your plan. Someone who will encourage, but also challenge your thinking.

## Reflective exercise

As you think about your career it is helpful to consider the questions below:

- Where do you get your energy from?
- What really excites you about life?
- What topics or causes invoke a deeply ingrained response in you?
- What are your core values?

Be true to yourself with your answers – don't fall into the trap of giving answers you think you should give, or answers that you think *other people* will approve of. Having written down the answers, ask yourself how you can construct a career that will embrace those attributes that include what is most important to you.

# 04
# Induction (as an employee)

The first few months in a new job are critical for success. While it is your new manager's job to provide everything you need in order to settle in to your new role quickly and effectively, there are also things you can do to ensure that you are making the most of the opportunities a new job presents.

## Early success priorities

Focus on setting yourself up for success. To do this, it is important to plan accordingly. In your early weeks, you should have three key priorities:

1 Build good relationships, especially with your boss, team and other key stakeholders.

2 Get very clear on what success looks like for you and your team – identify any risks.

3 Develop an understanding of the company culture and way of working.

The best way to make progress on these priorities is to ask questions and listen intently to the answers. Remember, you are trying to find out where you and your role fit within the big picture, and how your priorities align with the overall strategy. It is not unusual for people from different parts of the organization to have a different perspective on how your team makes an impact in the organization. In addition, you want to know who the key decision-makers are and who are the influencers.

There are several key pitfalls that new employees can easily fall into, including:

- Trying to demonstrate what they know, as opposed to listening.
- Not asking enough questions, either because they are making assumptions or because they're afraid of looking silly.
- Focusing on inputs rather than outputs – what they have to do, instead of what they have to achieve.
- Failing to clarify what success looks like and what is expected of them.
- Failing to build relationships with the right people, eg key stakeholders.
- Not fully utilizing the guidance and experience of a mentor (if provided).

## *Recognize the challenge*

Starting at a new company or job can be very unsettling. Inevitably, you will be taken out of your comfort zone and will have to establish yourself in the new role. You will have to learn how to work in the new situation, and you may well experience highs and lows throughout the process.

It can be helpful to focus on the following areas:

- **The company:** get to know the company strategy, culture, and key risks and opportunities that are expected over the next 12 months. What are the company goals and who are the key leaders that will determine whether the goals are achieved? How is good or bad news communicated within the company? How is disagreement managed within the company?
- **The stakeholders:** Who are your key internal and external clients? How do they contribute to your success and how do you contribute to their success? What will they expect from you? How do they like to be engaged? What are their working styles?
- **The team:** this applies to both your team (direct reports) and the team in which you operate (peers). Introduce yourself as both a professional and a person. How is your team viewed within the organization? What does your team want from you? What goals and priorities do other members of the team have? Do these differ from your own and do you need to be mindful of these while completing your own work? Explain to the team how you hope to grow and learn over your first 100 days.
- **The role:** What are your precise responsibilities? What is your decision-making empowerment? How are budgets set? Where does the role sit within the management hierarchy?
- **The success criteria:** What does success look like? How will it be measured? How will you and others know when you have reached your goals – what will be different? Be specific on both the hard and soft measures.

# The unwritten rules

In addition to formal procedures and policies, there will almost certainly be customs and practices that you will need to be aware of. Solicit information on the following:

- Email response times – in some companies there is an expectation that emails are responded to (or at least acknowledged) within 24 hours.
- Dress code, including:
  - jewellery;
  - uniform requirements;
  - visibility or otherwise of tattoos;
  - hairstyles and colours;
  - does the dress code vary if you are in a customer-facing role?
- Religion and politics – how are these expressed or practised? What is appropriate, legal, normal, accepted?
- Content and format of 'out of office' automated email responses.
- Expectation on attendance at after-work activities (formal and informal).
- The norms around alcohol consumption at company events.
- Travel and expenses policies.
- The use or otherwise of competitor products and services.
- When, how and where people take lunch breaks.
- Annual leave and national holidays – are there unwritten or official rules around who can take what days off and when? Blackout periods when no one can be away? Hierarchies where seniority gets first choice of days?
- Are there restrictions (or expectations) around the purchase and use of company products?
- 'Fraternization' or dating rules – formal or unspoken. Does the company have any rules on relationships with clients, customers, colleagues, peers, suppliers, etc?
- Are there any other peculiarities unique to your company that a new hire should be aware of?

## Tips, tricks and takeaways

- **Be constructive:** give due recognition for what impresses you. You will spot ways to improve how things work in the company or team, but be careful how you bring about change. Don't be overly critical of the past or current ways of doing things, focus your energy instead on what can be improved and the benefits that will accrue once the changes are made.

- **Self-reflection:** set a date with yourself to review your impact after 4–5 months. Reflect on your impact in the role – have you brought about change? Is the company or team doing better or perceived as doing better? What could you do differently now to improve your impact?

- **Keep records:** keep a record of your learning and experience over the first few months. At the very least, the next person to join the company will benefit from your experience.

- **Medical requirements:** make your boss aware of any underlying medical condition or allergies you may have, eg being diabetic or asthmatic.

- **Pre-determined commitments:** you may have made a personal commitment or booked a holiday prior to joining the company. If you haven't already, make your boss aware of any commitments on your first day, so that they can plan accordingly.

## Reflective exercise

Think about a new job you are going to start, or imagine that you are about to start your current job, but in another company. Write down the types of questions you want to ask. These questions should help you get an understanding of the context, the key priorities and future expectations of the role. Think about how you could plan to probe further, if you feel there is an underlying or unspoken factor impacting the answers you get.

Some examples to start you off might be:

- What is the desired culture of the team?

- How do you deal with conflict?

- What generally gives rise to stress in the team?

- What is the primary purpose of the team?

# 05
# Building good relationships

It is important to invest time in building relationships in the workplace. Nobody is an island – to be successful in the organization, you will need the support of others.

Below are some actions you can take that may help in setting your working relationships up for success.

## Take an interest in other people

It is helpful to know what is important to people both inside and outside of work. Being interested in your colleagues' priorities could help in understanding how to build or develop effective working relationships. If you have not met a colleague before, it may be a good idea to look at their LinkedIn profile, or ask others who may know them to give you some insight. At this point, you are simply looking for common ground or similar points of interest, as a foundation to a positive working relationship. Another way to find these things out is to create an opportunity to ask them to introduce themselves to you or the group. As they introduce themselves, you can listen for areas of common interest, or themes where you may share a similar perspective.

## Place yourself in the other person's situation

Try to have empathy, and seek to understand the other person's hopes, fears and aspirations as they take on a new role or begin to work with you. Rather than simply broadcasting your point of view to someone, focus on listening to them. What will be important to them? What do they need to know? What does success look like for them? It is important to put these questions to the individual soon after the relationship starts. This gives you the opportunity to offer help – a key building block in the development of a good relationship.

# Present yourself

It is important to make a good impression, and the best way to do so is to ask insightful questions, rather than simply demonstrating what you know. Remember, having knowledge is not an asset unless you can apply that knowledge – or in other words, use your knowledge to deliver impact in your role or help others make an impact in theirs. Ultimately, you want people to see you as an ally. Again, you can ask them about their hopes for the role and their priorities, and specifically what you can do to help them.

# Ways of working

Establish how the person likes to work and communicate – what are their likes and dislikes? Share with them your work preferences and style.

# A quick win

Help the individual to have an early 'win' so that they can build their confidence and trust in you. If they are new to the organization, you could introduce them to the culture and the key stakeholders. It may also be worth helping them to prioritize by sharing with them your view of high-priority challenges or opportunities facing the organization, and the history and context surrounding these issues.

# Be solution oriented

While it is helpful to point out pitfalls or issues to the person, it is also much more valuable to assist them with some well-thought-through suggestions or solutions.

If you are a manager of a new starter, read Chapter 32 to learn more about new employee induction and setting up the individual for success.

---

### Tips, tricks and takeaways

- **Assumptions:** Have you made assumptions? If you have worked with someone in the past and now find yourself working with them again, for example, don't assume that they haven't changed or taken on new interests.

- **Unconscious bias:** you may hear things about people before meeting them. When we meet new people, there is a tendency for our unconscious biases to kick in and influence our first impressions. This is entirely natural: these thought patterns are an evolutionary coping mechanism we use to make sense of our world, so they are very difficult to avoid. The very fact that these biases are unconscious makes it difficult for us to spot. The key is to notice when you think you may be being stereotypical or overly positive or negative in your first reaction to the individual – keep an open mind beyond that first impression, and let your relationship form based on actual experience instead of snap judgements.

- **Be careful with gossip:** in some office cultures, harmless gossiping is something that can help liven up conversations or simply fuel the human curiosity about how and why individuals do certain things. Some individuals will use gossip as a means of building a relationship – while this can be OK, or even positive, it is important that it is not a precursor to the building of a clique or setting the scene for more derogatory comments. Spreading gossip can be viewed very negatively as it is potentially a breach of trust, so tread warily.

## Reflective exercise

Review 'stale relationships'. Look at your LinkedIn connections, Facebook friends list, email contacts and so on – use this to pull together a rough list of people you know:

- How many of these have you met with in the last year?
- Who have you had any communication with in the last year – an email, phone call, text or social media interaction?
- How many of these have you deliberately distanced yourself from – are the reasons still true?
- How many have tried to be in communication with you?

If you did not consciously let the relationship lapse, then you could consider setting up meetings with those whom you have not seen recently, or dropping them a quick email to stay in touch

# 06
# Why mindset matters

Our mindset is a combination of the beliefs and feelings that determine our view or attitude to life. Our general wellbeing is heavily influenced by the choices we make, especially those we make relating to our attitude. This attitude to life underpins our demeanour, colours our thinking and determines our approach to life's opportunities and challenges.

Attitude also impacts how others engage with us, and can be the determining factor affecting a positive or negative dialogue. When individuals are dealing with a very difficult and stressful situation, that stress can be reduced if those involved bring a positive attitude to the table. Thus people are more likely to gravitate towards individuals with a positive attitude.

## Do you have a fixed or growth mindset?

The first step to changing your mindset begins with opening your mind to learning the possibilities of a situation. If we approach a situation with a view that our perspective is 'correct' and that others are 'wrong', then we are displaying what is referred to as a fixed mindset. If we retain a fixed mindset, then we will merely maintain the status quo – and nothing much will change. For some people this is OK, because they remain within their comfort zone; however, those people may well miss learning opportunities or opportunities to grow.

Those displaying what is referred to as a *growth* mindset see the present reality as a starting point. They then focus on what actions can be taken to learn and develop en route to achieving their goals. In other words, they focus on what is possible, without dwelling too much on the current situation (Dweck, 2006).

# How can I change my mindset?

The best way to change your mindset is to challenge yourself and surround yourself with people you can learn from. Engage positively to understand why others may hold a different perspective or viewpoint from yours – do this with the intent of learning and building upon your knowledge, as opposed to purely defending your own point of view.

The key components of a growth mindset are:

- self-awareness;
- a willingness to experiment;
- a focus on progress;
- learning opportunities.

## *Take ownership*

Some people will cast themselves in the role of victim, ie 'if only somebody else would do X then I would be happy'. In contrast, high-performing and happy people tend to recognize that they have what it takes within them to be successful. They take ownership and control of their situation and put a plan in place to achieve their goals. The trick is to build your action plan based upon what you can control and try to minimize over-reliance on luck or a third party. What would you do if you weren't afraid?

## *Self-awareness*

Recognize that we all see the world differently. Eye witnesses' accounts of the same event often show that people can go through the exact same experience and 'see' completely different things. This is because we all see the world through the prism of our own unique experience, values and preferences. We log in our memory the things that resonate with us, and dismiss other aspects of the experience that did not make an impact – so our reconstruction of reality will differ from another person's view of the same experience. This is not right or wrong, it is simply a different view of the world.

Once we recognize that others will see the world differently we can stop wasting time and energy trying to get them to see the world through our eyes. It is worth taking the time to build your self-awareness.

## A willingness to experiment

Occasionally we fall into the trap of passing judgement. Judgement implies right and wrong; it entails appointing ourselves as the knowledgeable one or the person with the 'right' point of view. Once we do this we subconsciously put ourselves into a position whereby we may have to defend our perspective. Ironically, we tend to pass judgement on those who are closest to us, thus running the risk of alienating a potential ally.

By choosing not to make a judgement we can open our minds to positive experiences. We must be continuously willing to experiment and see each outcome as a learning opportunity.

## Assess your perception of reality

You have a choice about how you react to and manage your feelings, in the same way that you can choose how you react to situations and behaviours. Take the time to question why you feel the way you do – can you change the way you feel by changing your perception of what has happened? For example, instead of looking at a micro view, look at the bigger picture. A great tip is to focus on progress rather than the immediate situation. If you encounter a block or setback, it is worth taking a step back and asking yourself what would have happened a month or a year ago – inevitably you will see that you have probably made great progress.

## Look for positive intentions

An individual's behaviour may irk you, but before you allow the annoyance to alter your mood look for an underlying positive intention. Don't allow the drama of the story to obscure the positive intent behind the message.

## Tips, tricks and takeaways

- **Self check:** you will know whether you are displaying a growth mindset if you can answer 'yes' to the following questions:
  - Are you challenging yourself?
  - Are you taking yourself out of your comfort zone?
  - Are you taking action, as opposed to talking about taking action?
  - Are you spending time searching for possibilities, as opposed to preserving the status quo?
- **Believe in yourself:** some of the world's most successful companies were founded in the depths of recessions – despite the prevailing sentiment, their founders saw opportunity. The companies or products below were all launched in the midst of recession:
  - *Fortune* magazine was launched in New York at an astronomical price (in relative terms) of $1 in 1929, in the middle of the Great Depression. Similarly, Revlon cosmetics was launched in 1932.
  - Microsoft (1975) and Apple (1976) were both founded in the middle of a recession.
  - General Electric was founded in 1892, a year before a major economic downturn.
  - Cirque du Soleil was founded in 1982, despite the circus industry being in steep decline and the recession of the 1980s being in full swing.
- **Have an open mind:** the examples above illustrate that opportunity can be found in the most unlikely of scenarios, but you have to have an open mind that is looking for the opportunity, as opposed to a fixed mindset that is simply resigned to one's fate.

## Reflective exercise

Make a list of actions you have taken or things you are doing differently as a result of what you have learnt over the last 12 months. If you are struggling to write a meaningful list of changes, it may indicate that you are operating with a fixed mindset.

When something doesn't go the way you originally expected do you reflect on what was learnt or what went wrong? The first may indicate more of a growth mindset, whereas the second may show a more fixed mindset.

# Reference

Dweck, C (2006) *Mindset: The new psychology of success*, Ballantine Books, New York

# 07
# Personal work–life balance

It is likely over the course of your career that you will work for more than 50 years in some guise or another – your career is the proverbial marathon not a sprint. Consequently, it is important to ensure that you are managing yourself in a way that will enable you to make a meaningful contribution to your work, your family, your community and your own personal ambitions. Work–life balance (WLB) is particularly challenging, as it inevitably involves the juggling of many apparently conflicting needs. Further complexity is introduced as those needs change over time, along with changes in your personal circumstances.

Nobody else can manage or own your work–life balance; you are the only person who can take the necessary steps. It is imperative that you own the process of putting in place a plan that will enable you to meet your personal as well as your work aspirations. Healthy work–life balance is all about behaviour, actions and habits.

Here are some helpful actions for you to take that will enable others assist you in achieving your work–life balance goals:

- Prioritize: make a list of what is most important to you.
- For each priority consider what constitutes a good work–life balance for you. Define 'success' for each of your priorities:
  o How will you know when you have a good work–life balance?
  o What will be different?
  o How will you feel?
  o How will others know when you are happy with your work–life balance?
- Set work–life balance goals:
  o Write down your WLB goals.
  o Share those goals with a partner or friend.

- It is important to develop your plan in conjunction with others as the big threats to work–life balance are inconsistency, ambiguity and a lack of support from team or family members.
- Before sharing your plan with your employer make sure you have checked the following:
  - o Is your role suitable for flexible working?
  - o Will there be a customer impact?
  - o What will the benefit be to your employer of accommodating your WLB needs?
- If possible, try to accommodate the needs of work colleagues in your plan.
- Be cognizant of the fact that your employer's business may require you to be flexible as customer requirements change, thus your plan should have a little contingency room.

## Be iterative

Work–life balance is highly personal and will probably vary as your life circumstances change. Consequently, it is a good idea to see work–life balance as a state that needs to be nurtured and re-evaluated over time. It is a good idea to put a reminder in your calendar to discuss your work–life balance with your boss every six months. The purpose of the review is to evaluate whether you are achieving your work–life balance goals.

You may from time to time make a decision to change aspects of your work and home life to meet specific short-term needs: it is perfectly OK to work late nights over a sustained period if you feel it will yield longer-term benefits; however, you should always be aware of the 'opportunity cost' of such a decision. Similarly, if you choose to work from home there may be an opportunity cost to being out of sight – you may miss out on opportunities.

## Be consistent

As we plan our schedules we all need an element of consistency. Some aspects of the weeks and months need to be predictable – specifically those aspects that pertain to our physical and mental health. Adequate sleep, exercise and 'me time' need to be planned into the schedule as non-negotiables.

You control and own this aspect of your work–life balance, so be sure to prioritize it accordingly. It is sometimes good to involve a third party when putting exercise and 'me time' into your schedule. For example, if you have a training partner or make a commitment to a friend to participate in an activity, it is much more difficult to cancel the activity if you will be letting somebody down.

# Be clear

Have you taken action to protect those elements of your schedule that you own? Ambiguity of expectation can be a source of stress for many people. Being very clear in setting expectations for the outputs or outcomes you expect from others will help them plan. Lack of clarity at the outset will inevitably lead to disappointment and the need for a last-minute scramble, which will inevitably impact work–life balance. Therefore, when taking on something new, begin with the end in mind – make sure you calibrate with other stakeholders on the specifics of the expectations and outcomes.

Lack of support from within the team and family can often be addressed by making them aware of what support you need, why you need it and what you will do in return for their assistance. Focus on the impact of the output rather than simply saying 'I need help'.

## Tips, tricks and takeaways

- **Be prepared:** as an individual, it is important to plan prior to a work–life balance discussion. Know what you need and why you need it. Ask yourself whether your work–life balance needs are reasonable. Above all, be able to show how you will deliver more for the company if your work–life balance needs are accommodated. You don't want your employer to conclude that they would be better off if you left and they hired someone else.

- **Plan ahead:** at the beginning of every year, put all important non-work dates (birthdays, anniversaries, parent–teacher meetings, holidays, medical and dentist appointments, etc) into your calendar with appropriate reminders set a week in advance so that you can book time off, buy a present, etc.

- **Consider all aspects:** make sure you have considered the following: your mental health; your physical health; time for meaningful engagement with good friends; time for community activity, volunteering or giving back; holidays; medical appointments; family time.
- **Planning tip:** look for opportunities to combine priorities or activities, eg you could exercise with a good friend, you could involve your partner and children in volunteering or you could set up some volunteering activities in work. Try to involve others in your activities, as the simple requirement to honour a commitment to another person will help you stay committed to the plan.

## Reflective exercise

Take time out to reflect on your work–life balance:

- Make a list of your priorities.
- Assess your work patterns:
  - Are you often the first to arrive *and* the last to leave?
  - Do you skip lunch?
  - Do you use your annual leave?
- Do others (friends, family and work colleagues) know how they can help your work–life balance?
- Do you go to the doctor or dentist promptly when you need to, even if it means taking time off work?
- Do you work when you're on holiday?

# 08
# Managing stress

Stress arises when the real or perceived demands on someone exceed their ability to respond to those demands in what they feel is an appropriate manner. It is very closely linked to a feeling of a loss of control over a situation, and can have a dramatic impact on both work performance and personal life. Successful organizations understand that they are only as strong as their people; a good company will actively pursue a policy endorsing a positive approach to mental health. There are several reasons for a company to care about the mental health and stress levels of their employees:

- They have a legal responsibility (under the Health and Safety at Work Act 1974) to ensure a healthy and safe working environment for their employees; this includes mental health.

- Companies who have a well-structured approach to managing and sustaining a thriving environment that is conducive to the positive mental health of their employees will see significant benefits in terms of commitment (talent retention) and productivity.

- Other benefits include enhanced morale, loyalty, employee engagement and even improved profitability.

- Many companies care about the moral and ethical responsibility of human beings to look out for one other – this is sometimes known as corporate social responsibility.

All this is to say that it is reasonable to expect your company to have a positive approach to helping you manage your stress level – and your mental health in general. While this chapter focuses on the actions you can take, a good company will not leave you to handle your stress alone.

# How to manage stress

Actions to deal with stress can be highly personal. The actions suggested in this chapter will have a greater or lesser impact depending upon the individual, so it is good to try more than one, so that you can identify what has the most powerful impact for you. In no particular order, you could try:

- Keeping a stress diary – identify causes and effects; prioritize causes relative to impact.

- Setting up a 'to do' list with appropriate categorization, to help you feel more in control of your work:
  - what is urgent;
  - what is important;
  - what is not important now;
  - what should be delegated to someone else.

- Planning your time well – keeping your calendar up to date, and allocating your time to certain tasks.

- Minimizing interruptions – for example, only check and respond to your email at certain times, and log off outside of these times; keep your phone on silent mode at work.

- Sharing your feelings with someone you trust. The old adage 'a problem shared is a problem halved' has a lot of truth in it; talking to someone to share your understanding of a scenario or challenge, and your feelings about it, can be quite cathartic.

- Focusing on what you can control. Don't allow your energy to be consumed with things you cannot control; always look for actions that are within your power, and focus on completing those actions. The process of completing the actions will give you a sense of progress and achievement, which may well help your stress.

- Using your commute to and from work to switch off:
  - listen to calming music;
  - read a book (or listen to an audiobook);
  - try to avoid radio talk shows or podcasts on topics that may add to your stress.

- Taking your breaks – don't eat your lunch at your desk; get up, leave the office and have some quiet time to yourself, or meet with a friend or colleague to talk about non-work topics. If you can combine this with a short walk, that would be even better!

- Get involved in clubs or societies (either within or outside of work) – it may sound counterintuitive to take on something additional if you are already feeling overwhelmed or stressed, but involvement in a group activity can be a very positive experience, which lifts one's mood.

- Trying some techniques that many people find helpful in good mental health practice:

  o  deep breathing;

  o  yoga;

  o  mindfulness;

  o  take exercise – even light exercise such as walking will help;

  o  talk about your feelings;

  o  avoid alcohol and drugs.

# What should I do if I think someone at work is under stress?

If you suspect that someone at your work is under an unmanageable level of stress, there are some actions you might consider taking – but, even if ultimately you can't do any more than listen to them, it is likely that they will appreciate the concern.

First, try to establish a connection with the person – if one doesn't already exist – and find a quiet place to ask the person open-ended questions about how they are feeling. Gently share your concerns and point out what you have noticed – have they been unusually snappy, for example? Or missing a lot of deadlines, which is unlike them? If they decide to talk to you about how they have been feeling, then show empathy, listen carefully and try not to appear to be judgemental in any way. Simply listen with understanding; it's probably not helpful to wade right in and try to solve their problem for them, rather you should try to help them identify the root cause of the issue themselves. Remember, stress is often linked to feeling out of control, and telling a stressed person 'how to fix it' may well make them feel worse.

Some common stress-causing factors are workload, lack of confidence (whether founded or unfounded) or difficulties with interpersonal relationships. Sometimes the person will already know the root of the problem, in which case just talking may be helpful for them – and sometimes the very act of having this conversation with you will kick-start the process of recovery for them. However, if you do speak to someone about their stress levels, don't expect an immediate impact. No matter how helpful the conversation, it probably took them some time to get to where they are now, and it will probably take them time to recover or get back to being themselves again. If appropriate, you could suggest some of the actions outlined in the section above.

One final thing: be aware of your own reactions and the impact of the discussion on you. It can be upsetting to understand how stressed someone is, and you may find yourself worrying about this person, so it is important that you remain aware of the impact of the conversation on you. Know your limits; at the end of the day there is only so much you can do, and ultimately everyone has to take ownership of their own stress and mental health. You can support them on their journey by offering encouragement and continuing to be there for them, but you should do this in a way that takes your own needs into consideration.

## Tips, tricks and takeaways

- **No one-size-fits-all:** there is no one-size-fits-all solution to stress or good mental health. Any action, solution, policy or initiative – no matter how well-meaning – must take into account the different needs of different people and the circumstances in which they operate. What works for one person may not work for another.

- **Culture:** the culture of an organization can hugely influence the mental health of its workforce. It is important for a leader to raise the topic of mental health and make people aware of the support that is in place.

- **Stigma:** unfortunately, there is still a stigma associated with mental health challenges in many cultures. Be aware that the people around you may not feel comfortable letting on that they feel stressed, and do what you can to encourage a culture of acceptance and non-judgement.

- **Balance:** physical and mental health go hand in hand – looking after your physical wellbeing can have a dramatically positive impact on your stress management.

- **Work social events:** many work cultures include activities or events designed to let the team relax and unwind together. Sometimes those events revolve around alcohol and gatherings in pubs and restaurants; ironically, such events could in fact contribute to someone's stress, if they feel pressured to participate, or drink more than they want to (or at all). Alcohol is not always welcome, wanted or helpful, so when planning or requesting off-site activities, consider something that does not include alcohol or put people under pressure.

- **Life events:** no matter how resilient an individual, significant life events can and do take their toll on one's stress levels. Births, deaths, marriages, divorce, moving house, health issues and many other aspects of life can all be stressful. Your reaction to these things may even come as a surprise to you, so it is important to reflect and take stock as appropriate.

- **Access to advice:** access to advice and support is important for prevention of stress. Could your workplace invite in professionals to give talks on appropriate topics? Is there an EAP (employee assistance plan)? Is financial counselling available from the company's pension provider?

## Reflective exercise

It's good to be aware of your own moods, patterns, and stress levels and triggers. Try this:

- Keep a mood diary for a few days, or even a few weeks. Write down whenever you feel particularly happy, stressed, sad or angry – what time, what is happening, what you have eaten and drunk, and any other details that might contribute. Do you notice any patterns?

- Do a wellbeing 'self-audit'. How is your exercise? Your diet? Do you have a healthy and consistent work–life balance? Are you finding enjoyment and fulfilment in your job? In your personal life? How is your sleep?

# 09
# Dealing with disappointing news at work

As an employee you will encounter situations where you get disappointing news, for example if you get passed over for a promotion, you don't get the pay rise you were expecting or you receive disappointing performance feedback. In such situations it is important to react in a professional manner. The last thing you want to do is convey the impression that you can't handle bad news, or worse still you react badly when you don't get your own way.

In situations such as these, it is perfectly reasonable to acknowledge the reality and have an unemotional, controlled conversation with your boss to express your disappointment. Resist the temptation to gossip. Be aware of your body language – sometimes you may be voicing all the right things, but your facial expressions and body language tell a different story. Ultimately, you want to turn the situation into a personal learning experience.

## Being passed over for a promotion

There are almost always positives that can be gleaned from any situation. Take the time for some quiet, balanced reflection and to be honest with yourself. If you have been passed over for a promotion, you should ask yourself the following questions:

- Why did I get passed over? Always seek feedback from HR or the hiring manager and *own* the actions arising from the feedback – ie come up with a reason that is actionable by you. There is little value in focusing on the actions of others, or apportioning blame (even if it is true), as you can't control how others act. You *can* control your own actions, so this is where it is valuable to focus.

- What can I learn from the person who was appointed to the role?
- What can I gain from supporting the person who was appointed to the role?

There may also be harder questions to ask: for example, does being passed over for a promotion indicate that the management team feel you have reached a plateau in your career, or that you are not displaying the competencies required for the role? Remember, there is a huge difference between having the required competencies and displaying the required competencies. At this point you need to be honest with yourself – do you have the required skills and competencies? More importantly, do you use the skills and competencies to benefit the company or team?

It is important to get an understanding of what skills you need to gain and what behaviours you need to exhibit. It is fair and reasonable to ask your boss for feedback on what you would need to do to be successful if such an opportunity came up again in the future. At the very least, you need to come up with answers to the following:

- What do you do well?
- What two or three things should you do differently to have greater impact?

# Receiving disappointing or negative feedback

First, look for the positives when you are presented with critical feedback. If someone takes the time to give you negative feedback they are doing a few things:

- They are showing that you are worth investing in.
- They are showing that they think you are strong enough to take the feedback.
- They are being courageous – ie they may be telling you something others have not had the courage to share with you.
- They are taking an interest in you, they are showing they care. Remember, the easy option would be for the individual to say nothing.

Feedback is never right or wrong (or arguably, good or bad); it is almost always someone's opinion. By definition, an opinion cannot be right or wrong. So, it can be helpful to remember that it is your choice how you react!

If you get disappointing feedback it can be helpful to follow the process below:

- Ask yourself: 'why did I get this feedback?'
  - o Is the feedback reasonable?
  - o Is it the feedback I did not like, or the manner in which it was delivered? It is important to differentiate between the core feedback and the behaviour exhibited by the person giving the feedback.
  - o Is the feedback balanced? Did the person delivering the feedback recognize what you did well, as well as what could be improved?
  - o Always own the answer – again, don't fall into the trap of seeing yourself as a victim. Come up with a reason that is within your control, and avoid the temptation to blame the person giving you the feedback or conclude too quickly that they are 'wrong'.
- Seek out a trusted third party to share your feelings and experience:
  - o Discuss the feedback – see if the other person shares the same perspective, or can see how the person who gave you the feedback may have formed their view.
  - o Share your feelings about the feedback – it is OK to be upset, and sometimes it is helpful to talk about it.
- Ask yourself 'if I was in the situation again what would I have done differently?'
- Speak with the person who gave you the feedback to check your learning and understanding. Let them know that you have reflected on what they told you, and share with them what you have learnt or decided to change. Check whether this is consistent with what they meant – this way you will avoid any misunderstandings, and highlight any positive changes.
- Ask them to continue to give you feedback, and let them know you are grateful. However, if the feedback was delivered in an unhelpful or hurtful way, it may be good at this point to let them know how this affected you, and ask them if they could deliver feedback differently in future. For example, if you were pulled up in public on something you were doing wrong, and this was embarrassing, you may want to thank them for bringing the problem to your attention, but also ask that they speak to you privately in future.

- Finally – especially if the feedback was from your boss – it will be important to agree on what success looks like for future deliverables.

If, having taken the steps above, you still feel the feedback was unreasonable, then you have to reflect and decide what you want to do in the longer term:

- Is there a gap between what you expect of yourself and what this person expects of you? If so, how might this gap be closed?

- Is this just their opinion? What would be the impact of deciding to let them have that opinion, but not change what you're doing?

- Does the person giving you feedback have a significant impact on your career progression or day-to-day happiness?

There may also be a harder message – strongly negative feedback may indicate that you are not displaying the competencies required for the role. Whether or not you feel this is true, concerns around your competency for your role are worth taking seriously. Be honest with yourself – do you have the required skills and competencies? More importantly, do you use the skills and competencies that you have effectively? Is the feedback coming from your boss?

It is important to get an understanding of what competencies you need to gain, and what behaviours you need to exhibit. It is fair and reasonable to ask your boss for feedback on what you need to do to be successful. When you have received strongly disappointing feedback it can be tempting not to invite more, but if you aren't clear on what you actually need to do to improve, the situation won't change, so asking for specific and constructive feedback is important.

### Tips, tricks and takeaways

- **Be balanced:** ask for time and space to make a considered response. An emotive response in the heat of the moment probably won't come across as professional so take the time to reflect and come back with a thoughtful perspective. It is OK to ask for more detail on the feedback specifically as it pertains to you. Try to avoid comparisons to others if at all possible.

## Reflective exercise

Think about the last time you were disappointed at work. What happened? Why was it disappointing?

   If you can, note down:

- Three things you would handle differently to improve how you handled the disappointment.

- Three things you learnt from the situation.

- One thing you have changed as a result of the disappointing situation.

# 10
# Resilience

The word resilience comes from the Latin word '*resili*' meaning the ability to spring back or adapt to a new environment. To be resilient we must manage our thoughts, feelings and behaviours so that we can remain open to learning and adapting throughout the experience.

A resilient person will always ask 'How can I make the best of the situation?' rather than dwelling on the nature of the disappointment. In other words, they acknowledge the reality and deal with the setback in a positive manner, taking ownership of making the best of the situation.

It is important to note that resilience is not necessarily universal; it is not a trait that you have or don't have. Individuals who are generally considered to be resilient may not react in a resilient manner in all circumstances, thus high achievers can sometimes be shocked when they encounter a seemingly trivial situation where their resilience does not emerge. Typically, a successful entrepreneur will have had to deal with many setbacks and much disappointment before they become successful. They develop and display resilience in the early days to get their business off the ground; however, that does not mean they will be resilient in all situations. Occasionally a minor setback can induce a loss of confidence that undermines their resilience.

## How can you boost your resilience?

Resilience can be developed and learnt over time. There is no single approach to managing resilience, but the following can be helpful:

- **Share the concern or experience:** the old adage 'a problem shared is a problem halved' has a lot of truth. It is always good to talk to another person and share your thoughts and feelings about the topic that is concerning you or causing you stress and anxiety. Make sure the person you talk to is an appropriate person – a friend, partner or professional mentor may be more appropriate than your direct manager, for example, or in some cases, your direct manager may be more appropriate than a friend.

- **Focus on what you can control:** no matter how insignificant the action appears, it is always good to do something within your control that will help alleviate some of the stress of the situation. By focusing on what you can control, you take ownership for that part of the situation and can directly influence a positive outcome. By taking an action, you remove the risk of casting yourself in the role of victim. By focusing on what you can control, you are applying your energy to a positive endeavour as opposed to wasting energy on something you cannot control.

- **Reflect upon previous tough experiences:** invariably we have all experienced some level of trauma in the past – think back to those events and remind yourself of how you survived and got through that difficult situation. How have you dealt with stressful situations in the past? Can any of what you have learnt from previous challenges be applied to the current issue?

- **Take care of yourself:** to be resilient you need to look after yourself both physically and mentally. Take the time to reflect and think about what you need – sometimes it is OK to be selfish. Sleep, diet and exercise all impact our ability to be resilient.

- **Practise optimism and positive self-talk:** we can influence our own demeanour simply by talking ourselves up or down. Remind yourself of all that is good in your life and how you can (and do) make a positive contribution to your own life and the lives of others. You have assets and you bring those strengths to the situation you find yourself in – now is not the time to be self-critical. To help boost your mood try the following:

  o Do good things for other people.

  o Appreciate the world around you.

  o Develop and bolster relationships.

  o Establish goals that can be accomplished.

  o Choose to accept yourself, flaws and all.

- **Posture:** Are you acting with confidence? People around you will be taking their cues from your body language – a smile, or lack thereof, can send multiple messages to those around you. If you stand tall and smile people will gravitate towards you and take strength from your apparent confidence.

- **Realistic goals:** Are you setting yourself unrealistic goals?

Are you adding to your stress, thus undermining your resilience, by delivering outcomes that others don't value? For example, your customer or client may be very happy with a simple answer, but you instead spend a huge amount of time and energy delivering a magnificent comprehensive detailed response. In the eyes of the recipient, it contains a lot of 'nice to haves' rather than essential content, meaning that in practical terms, your over-delivery is of little value.

Do you routinely calibrate what success looks like with your boss/clients or customers *before* you embark on a piece of work?

## Am I lacking resilience?

A lack of resilience is usually characterized by the following:

- **Seeing yourself as a victim:** if you cast yourself in the role of the victim then you run the risk of creating a feeling of helplessness, which suggests that you may not be well disposed to taking positive action to improve the situation. The key trait of resilience is to focus on what you can control and take ownership of your actions.

- **Overreacting:** Do you find yourself overreacting to the small things? It is important to see events in the context of the big picture and to retain your sense of perspective. Your reaction to a small event can be telling in terms of your resilience: allowing something small to cloud the whole picture may indicate that your resilience is waning.

- **Persistent pessimism:** seeing only what is wrong and having a 'glass half empty' mindset can be energy-sapping and may lead to fatigue. For example, you give an excellent presentation and the audience responds very favourably with positive feedback, but when you are asked how it went you say 'we had a problem with the technology, which delayed the beginning of the presentation by five minutes'. Factually, this may be accurate – but it is not the important point.

- **Look for the positives:** it is much easier and more energizing for those around you to build upon a positive than address a negative. Specifically, as a leader it is important to remember people want to *feel* that they are progressing towards a positive outcome. Your role is to inspire them to take the journey to get a better outcome – that means focusing on the endpoint, rather than wallowing in a negative disposition.

- **Personalizing the event:** it is great to take ownership of a situation; however, if you always personalize the blame for a failure then you may be missing the fact that there are always wider factors impacting the outcome that you cannot control. Sometimes you have to recognize that external factors beyond your control will have an impact and you just have to acknowledge the reality.

- **Jumping to (negative) conclusions:** if an individual is struggling with a deliverable, you assume that they do not have what it takes to be successful, rather than concluding that they may actually be very good but just have not been given the appropriate support.

- **Succumbing to self-fulfilling prophesies:** similar to above, if we imagine the worst but do not prepare for the worst then we can run the risk of allowing a negative outlook to become a self-fulfilling prophesy. Maintain a positive vision as much as possible.

---

## Tips, tricks and takeaways

- **Let go of the little things:** don't overload yourself with trivial decisions if you are in a challenging situation. Allow someone else to make the trivial decisions while you focus on the big items that can help bring about a positive change.

- **Avoid comparisons:** comparisons are odious because you never have the full picture. You know everything about your own situation, but you never have the full picture of what is going on for the individual against whom you are comparing yourself. Comparison to others should never be your primary focus. You will always find people who are apparently more successful/happy/wealthy/popular, so it is pointless making comparisons.

- **Don't rain on your own parade!** Avoid perfectionism. Most of your stakeholders/customers want their needs met, not perfection. In our coaching experience, we often find that the pressure our clients are under is self-inflicted – either they set themselves an ultra-high (and often unattainable) bar, or they measure themselves against criteria that are not materially significant.

## Reflective exercise

Are you looking after yourself? Create a log of the following:

- Your hours of sleep.
- What, when and how you eat – on the go, on your own or sitting down with others?
- Your exercise.

Plot in the log what would be ideal for you in each category. Share the contents with a third party. Make an agreement with that person that you will sustain your good habits and make any necessary changes.

# 11
# Managing your personal brand

In everyday life we encounter brands at every turn, from food to cars to technology. In many cases, the brand 'values' of the product or service we encounter evoke a reaction within us. As a result, we create an affinity with a brand – we have our favourites, those we avoid, those we tolerate and those for which we have a neutral opinion.

As individuals developing a career we need to be cognizant of our own brand image. What would you like to be known for? What do you want to evoke in others when they engage you in person or online through your social media profile or blog posts?

## Why do I need a brand?

In today's competitive world you may want to stand out from the crowd or differentiate yourself from the competition. You may want your brand to reflect your reputation for creativity, your ability to be an effective problem-solver, or perhaps you want to be known as a subject matter expert in an industry sector or on a chosen topic.

Ultimately a strong brand will not only help you to get noticed, but it will help you get noticed for the right reasons. If you don't think about your brand and how it is perceived, you may end up with a 'default' brand, or be pigeonholed in a position that can limit your personal or professional growth.

## How to develop your brand

In developing your brand it is important that you are true to yourself and your abilities, and create an authentic brand image. Never be tempted to create a false persona, as this will open you to the risk of being exposed as a fraud and, in all likelihood, induce stress and confusion at a later stage. Over time people will get to know you, and if your brand image is fake they may begin to distrust you.

The first step in creating your brand image will centre on your self-awareness. People connect with people, not personas. People like to engage with authentic people who have values, hopes and fears like themselves.

## Step 1: self-awareness

Create your brand foundation by answering the questions below:

- What are your values?
- What do you believe in?
- What do you stand for?
- What are you truly passionate about?
- Where do you get your energy from?
- What is it that gives you most satisfaction?
- What are your personality traits?

Take the time to carefully consider your answers to the questions above, as they will form the bedrock of your brand image. Remember to be human – we all have vulnerabilities and needs, and there is no need to have a brand that makes you out to be perfect. You want people to be able to relate to you, empathize with you and be inspired by your actions.

## Step 2: tell your story

Using the answers to the questions in Step 1, create your story:

- What is it about you that you want to convey to others when they meet you or encounter you online?
- What do you want to be known for?
- What do you want others to see and feel when they engage you – either in person or online?

The core content of your story is contained in the answers you wrote in Step 1. In this step we are simply turning those answers into a paragraph or two that sums you up. In conjunction with this, have an 'elevator pitch' version of the story – something you can deliver in a few short sentences for maximum effectiveness.

## Step 3: who is your target audience?

Take the time to identify the individuals or groups that you feel will be interested in your story:

- Who is it that you want to influence?
- Why will they be interested in what you have to offer?
- What do you bring to your target audience that will catch their attention?
- What is it about you that may make it more likely for your target audience to respond or engage positively?

## Step 4: share your draft brand profile

It is important to try to get feedback on your desired brand before you publicize it. Friends and family can provide feedback, but a trusted mentor or coach will most likely give you more valuable feedback. If possible, try to get some feedback from someone who does not know you well, as their judgement won't be clouded by their knowledge of you and will give you a better understanding of how a stranger may react to your brand. Once you have refined your brand following the feedback you receive, you will be ready to put yourself out there. Go do it!

## Step 5: raising your brand profile

Now that you have decided upon your story and your target audience you can take the first steps in raising your brand profile. Think of the best method(s) of engaging your target audience. You may choose to leverage a number of channels simultaneously or consecutively. Essentially, you want to choose a medium that will enable you to stand out from the crowd and be compelling to your target audience.

Online:

- Build a website and optimize it effectively – this can hugely enhance your online profile as your website will appear in searches for you or topics related to your brand.
- Write or contribute to blogs.
- Create YouTube videos, podcasts and other engaging methods of delivering your message.
- Post relevant and regular content on your social media accounts.
- Maintain an updated LinkedIn profile.

Traditional media:

- Write articles for magazines or industry journals.
- Write articles for newspapers.
- Be a panellist or expert contributor on radio shows.

In-person activities:

- Speak at conferences.
- Hold one-to-one meetings with key stakeholders.
- Join and contribute to industry bodies or associations.
- Attend and speak at networking events.
- Nominate others, or have others nominate you, for industry awards.

## Tips, tricks and takeaways

- **Profiles and consistency:** don't forget that you are the owner of multiple profiles – an in-person profile, a LinkedIn profile, a Facebook profile, further social media profiles, a contributor profile to blogs, and so on. It is vitally important to have consistency in your branding, so align your postings and actions to your brand at all times. Remember that people who are interested in you will do social media searches to find out more about you, often before they even make contact with you.

- **Professional photo:** if you are creating the brand image of a serious business executive, it is probably not a good idea to have a profile picture of you from a boozy night out. Use a picture that reinforces your desired brand image. It is worth investing in a professional photo for your profile picture, or at a minimum using a photo taken for the purpose with a proper camera. No selfies or cropped holiday snaps for this one!

- **Stay relevant:** be sure that you keep your brand relevant and up to date – we live in a fast-paced world and if you don't show that you can keep pace with change, you run the risk of giving the impression that you are out of touch.

## Reflective exercise

1 Ask a friend or colleague to write down three words to describe you, or ask them what they think is your brand.

2 What are you known for?

3 What would you like to be known for?

4 What do you think are your growth areas or areas that you would like to develop so that you can include them the next time you refine or edit your brand?

5 Does your brand reflect what gets you *really excited* about life?

6 Do a 360-degree feedback exercise with the guidance of a coach or mentor.

The purpose of the exercise above is to identify the characteristics or traits that others see in you that you may not see in yourself.

# 12
# Effective networking

Networking is the process of growing the number of people with whom you have a positive working or social relationship. Specifically, you would like the people in your network to think of you when they come across information that may be of use to you or hear of an opportunity and connect you with that opportunity.

Remember, networking is a two-way street. Your value in the network is enhanced when you connect others to information that may be beneficial to them. Networking is usually a long-term play – you build relationships and facilitate connections. You may not be the short-term beneficiary, but by positively engaging with others you increase the likelihood of opportunities coming your way.

Networking is not selling. Networking is building mutually beneficial relationships that may or may not lead to an opportunity being realized in the future. If you approach it purely as a sales activity then you run the risk of alienating others or conveying a disingenuous purpose to the potential relationship (ie I am only in it for what I can get out of it).

Your first objective in networking is simply to ask those who are of most interest to you to meet for a follow-up over a cup of coffee.

## Why do I need to network?

You don't know what you don't know! You only have one set of eyes and ears, thus the amount of research you can do to find opportunities is limited. Your network acts as extra sets of eyes and ears for you, picking up information and identifying opportunities when you are not in the room.

The bottom line is, many opportunities for business development or career enhancement are initiated or spread by word of mouth. With career opportunities in particular, it is estimated that in more than 50 per cent of the cases, senior positions are likely to emerge through your network. Furthermore, many opportunities are never made public because the need was met by someone known to the hiring manager, so the opportunity was never advertised.

Human nature is positively disposed to personal references or recommendations, and it gives the person doing the hiring a sense of comfort if they feel they can trust the source of the recommendation. Think of opportunities as being like fish in the sea – if you have a small net, the likelihood of you catching many fish is low and it is impossible for you to catch a big fish; If you have a big net, your probability of catching fish increases dramatically and your ability to catch a big fish is greatly improved.

# How do I start networking?

There are two forms of networking: internal networking (which is particularly important if you work in a large company) and external networking.

## *Internal networking*

This is the process of building relationships with people who may now, or sometime in the future, be in a position to help you. In essence, you are expanding your profile and reach within the organization.

The best way to commence networking internally is to do some of the following:

- Get a mentor.
- Ask for advice on something you are working on from a third party with whom you would not normally work.
- Volunteer to get involved in projects or initiatives that will involve working with people from outside your team.
- Attend social events, join clubs and societies (set up a club or society if none already exist).
- Meet people for lunch or coffee.
- Offer to help others.

### *External networking*

This is the process of building relationships outside of your company with people who may now, or sometime in the future, be in a position to help you. In essence, you are expanding your profile and reach outside of the organization.

The best way to commence networking externally is to do some of the following:

- Be active and post articles on LinkedIn.
- Join industry associations.
- Write an article for an industry publication.
- Write a blog.
- Volunteer for charities.
- Attend conferences – or better still, speak at conferences.
- Join industry think tanks.
- Join university alumni groups.

In both types of networking you are listening to see how you can help, by joining the dots and making connections for others. That may be as simple as making an introduction to another person, or forwarding an article you come across at a later date, or simply sharing your own experience.

# Networking introductions

When asked by a third party what it is that you do, either as a company or as an individual, weigh up the balance between information, value and need. Read the sample good and bad answers below, as well as the explanations and suggestions for improvement:

- **Answer A:** 'I run a business making widgets. We are doing really well at the moment, our new product/service is very popular, we have double-digit growth and are planning to expand overseas in the short term.'

  **Verdict:** Not great, because it does not mention your unique value proposition; it does not say what you need; it gives the impression that you are very busy and run the risk of overstretching yourself; and the third party leaves the conversation not knowing how they can help.

- **Answer B:** 'I run a business making widgets. Our unique value proposition is we can make multi-coloured widgets to order. We are doing well at the moment as our new product/service is popular and we are growing, but we would like to diversify our customer base, and specifically be more attractive to potential customers in the pharma industry.'

  **Verdict:** Good, because you concisely convey your unique value proposition; you outline what you need or where you may like help; it gives the impression that you are doing well and are growing in a controlled fashion; and the third party leaves the conversation knowing how they can help.

- **Answer C:** 'I am the marketing director of a business making widgets. We are doing really well at the moment. Our new product/service is very popular, we have double digit growth and are planning to expand overseas in the short term. I am really excited about the long-term prospects.'

  **Verdict:** Not great, because it does not mention your unique value proposition; it does not say what you are open to in the future; it gives the impression that you are very busy, happy in your current role and potentially not interested in looking at other opportunities; the third party leaves the conversation not knowing how they can help.

- **Answer D:** 'I am the marketing director of a business making widgets. We are doing well at the moment. My passion is opening up new markets and developing online marketing strategies. Our new product/service is very popular, we can clearly see the link between the product growth and the implementation of the marketing strategy. I do enjoy the job and the company has been good to me, but I realize the importance of continuous learning and the need to take on new challenges.'

  **Verdict:** Good, because you concisely convey your unique value proposition; you outline what you like; it gives the impression that you are doing well and are open minded about the future; you do not specifically say that you are looking for a job; the third party leaves the conversation knowing that you may be open to considering other opportunities.

Unless you are comfortable knowing that the fact that you are job searching might get back to your current employer, you should never explicitly mention this in a networking scenario. If your current workplace knows you are job searching and are supportive, however, there is less risk in mentioning it.

## Tips, tricks and takeaways

- **Be vocal:** when you are in touch with your network, make them aware of how they can help you. In many cases people are so focused on the task at hand that they forget to tell you what they need. The impact is that that person walks away not knowing how they can help you or, worse still, gets the impression you are overloaded and can't take on more business.

- **Actively listen to the needs of others:** make a note of who you have met and how you could help them – and how they could help you in the future.

- **Keep your network current:** review your network (every six months) to ensure that you are keeping it current. If you haven't engaged with an individual for 12 months or more, then the relationship is probably dormant at best.

## Reflective exercise

Make a list (or set up a spreadsheet) of people you know and could be of assistance to you in your career. Alternatively, you could use the 'Friends' or 'Connections' lists on your Facebook or LinkedIn profiles, if you have them. Once you have your list, ask yourself these questions:

- When was the last time I made contact with this individual?
- What can I do to help this individual?
- Have I made this individual aware of either what is new about me or what they could to do help me?

NB: put a reminder in your calendar to repeat this exercise every six months.

If you were given the opportunity to meet with three or four people from your network in the next month, who would you choose and why?

Now: what is preventing you from setting up a meeting, or making contact with these people? Really challenge yourself: is the barrier to connecting real, or self-imposed?

# 13
# Leadership

Is leadership an art or a science? Leadership is a topic that remains a question in the minds of academics and coaches – is there a magic formula, or a prescriptive guide to becoming a successful leader? Well, no – but in my view, there are some characteristics that are common to all successful leaders. Everyone can be a leader if they put their mind to it, regardless of specific leadership style. (Indeed, a successful leader will need to be able to demonstrate a number of styles as they encounter different scenarios.)

## What makes a good leader?

The primary characteristics and behaviours of a strong leader are:

- vision and sense of purpose;
- integrity;
- authenticity;
- clarity;
- recognizing others;
- developing and promoting leadership in others;
- building community;
- confidence.

### Vision and sense of purpose

*Key attributes: future-oriented, knowing what it is they stand for and/or want to achieve and having the focused drive, energy, passion and courage to pursue their goals.*

People will follow individuals with great, well-formulated ideas, especially if those ideas are based upon a realistic prospect of success and are aligned to the followers' core values. A leader who has taken the time out to discover their true purpose will probably end up being more inspiring than an individual who has simply had a title bestowed upon them. You don't need a title to be a leader.

## Integrity

*Key attributes: self-aware, learner, open minded, empathy, integrity, including ethics.*

Strong leaders will be very self-aware, have the emotional intelligence and integrity to approach situations in a balanced manner. We all know that nobody is perfect, and good leaders prudently solicit help from those who have the skills or competencies that they do not have.

More and more high-calibre people are looking to work with leaders who demonstrate that they have high ethical standards. It is critical in the area of integrity and ethics that the leader is seen to 'walk the walk and talk the talk'. Integrity and ethics are not passive or covert traits; they must be publicly demonstrated – especially when times are tough or when the team faces a difficult decision.

## Authenticity

*Key attributes: trust and behaviours consistent with core values.*

A key part of your authenticity is to challenge team members to leave their comfort zone or to inspire others to achieve what they did not think was possible. In order to initiate the move out of the comfort zone, the leader must empathize with the team members as they face the challenge. Displaying emotions or feelings is core to being an authentic leader; just ensure you do so with composure, as composure inspires confidence. Failing is a necessary part of learning, and as a leader you will have to work with your team to devise appropriate methods to pilot new ideas in a safe environment. A good barometer is to ask yourself how many pilots you have run or enabled in the last 24 months. If the answer is none or a few, then you are probably at risk of stagnating in your comfort zone.

## Clarity

*Key attributes: clear on vision, goals and expectations.*

It is important as a leader to demonstrate a focused drive, energy and passion for your goal or vision. Ensure that your goals are clear and prioritized;

successful leaders always retain their focus on the primary goal and don't let themselves get distracted by secondary or 'nice to have' goals. The value of the secondary goals is diminished if the key priorities are not achieved, so focus is important.

Ambiguity can derail a team very quickly or be the source of discontent within the team. The leader must be very precise and clear when it comes to outlining the success factors for the team, and it is essential that these expectations are established early and clearly.

Providing clarity on goals and expectations is a critical aspect of leadership. It is important to have objectively measurable goals, as well as providing clarity on the behavioural norms that are expected from the team members. Clarity on the behavioural norms becomes critical when the team encounters a crisis or a decision that will require compromise. The leader is responsible for creating the environment within which team members can do their best work.

## Recognizing others

*Key attributes: demonstrate valuing others, listening.*

Strong leaders will be vigilant in looking for opportunities to recognize the contributions of others on the team. In this regard the leader will listen intently to what people are saying, all the time looking for opportunities to build on or incorporate a team member's ideas into the strategy. Additionally, they will listen for signs of underlying concerns that may be hindering a team member.

Prime motivators for people tend to revolve around doing meaningful work, making an impact and being recognized for their impact or contribution to the team. A good leader will construct their teams so that the individuals have the opportunity to perform to the best of their ability and the team delivers more than the sum of the parts.

Recognition is critical in sustaining positive behaviours and performance. The very act of noticing and recognizing the contribution or effort of the team members can be very motivational. Even seemingly inconsequential awards can have a very positive impact on the morale of the team. For low-performing team members, the simple act of recognizing that they have the potential to succeed may bring about the desired change in performance. The leader must take every opportunity to publicly and privately demonstrate that they value the contribution of individuals on the team.

## Developing and promoting leadership in others

*Key attributes: identify and develop talent within the team, support others with their personal goals, delegate certain aspects of leading to others.*

A strong leader will recruit high-calibre individuals onto the team. In fact, it could be argued that the leader's most significant contribution to the team is the selection and retention of the talent on the team. The challenge is that high-calibre individuals will always want to develop and invariably have other personal goals that they are trying to achieve. Remember, high performers will always be in demand; therefore, it is important for you as the leader to make your team an attractive place to work. Giving team members the appropriate experience and exposure will be important in the quest to retain talent on the team. Assisting team members with their own needs and broader goals is critical. Team members will most likely be appreciative of the opportunity to learn and grow, and in return will deliver more for the team in the long run.

Good leaders create other leaders, *not* followers, therefore a strong leader will provide team members with the opportunity to take the lead on certain aspects of the initiative or project. This leadership will be publicly visible and allow the individual to get the appropriate recognition if their work is good. Remember, if their work is not good then you as the leader need to take accountability for the poor work. By giving the team member the opportunity to lead, you are taking a risk and as such you are ultimately accountable for the outcome. Invariably, if you set the individual up for success (ie put in place guard rails or early warning signals) it is unlikely that the team member will fail and they will ultimately be very appreciative of the opportunity to lead.

Successful leaders look for the learning opportunity in the situation and set about using the lessons learnt to advance their cause. They will always create space for continuous professional development.

## Building community

*Key attributes: promote a sense of belonging to the team or a cause, enabling team members to be successful and do their best work.*

A person's sense of self-worth or even identity can be very strongly influenced by the experiences they have within the team. We have a natural instinct or desire to belong to a community of like-minded individuals who share similar values and hopes and fears for the future. A good leader will foster a sense of attachment and belonging to the team. Even if some individuals on the team work remotely or on very unique aspects of the initiative, it is important to make them feel they belong to a bigger collective and ensure that they do not feel isolated.

A key part of making people feel included is to solicit and incorporate their opinions and ideas into the team strategy or protocols. The leader must not only be open to taking on new ideas but also be curious enough to invite diverse perspectives.

The team will, in all likelihood, want to be part of creating the solution. They will want to feel ownership for (or at least have influence over) some of the final solution. High-performing teams do not like to be spoon fed, they like the challenge of figuring out how to achieve the goal.

## Confidence

*Key attributes: not afraid to take risks and make tough decisions.*

Successful leaders tend to know what they want, why they want it, and have a rough plan of how they are going to achieve their goals. They need to have the confidence to share their vision and plans and take feedback where appropriate. While it is good to have a rough plan, it is important not to be too prescriptive as a leader – this is where many leaders fall down.

Strong leaders always take action. Your energy and passion can be infectious within the team; in fact if you fail to be public in expressing your unwavering commitment to the cause those around you may lose confidence in you. A leader will be a change agent – they will not simply react to the environment, they will actively look to control their own and their group's destiny.

The leader needs to be comfortable with controlled experimentation or change that will advance the organization towards its goals. The change may simply reinvigorate an existing process, but the reinvigoration will energize the team and sustain progress, which is critical in a multi-year initiative. An audacious vision or goal will not be easy to achieve, so as the leader you must show the courage of your convictions and be willing to make sacrifices to achieve the goal. These sacrifices will become evident as you prioritize your time and energy. You display confidence by sharing what lies behind the courage of your convictions.

Very few leaders will escape having to make tough decisions or avoid taking risks. Therefore, it is important that you have the confidence and courage of your convictions to persevere in the face of adversity. The team will watch the leader and gain confidence from their conviction and determination to succeed. As a result, it is important that the leader *displays* their confidence.

People are not naturally resistant to change; however, people do resist if there is a real or perceived threat to their intrinsic values, sense of purpose or how they are rewarded. First and foremost, the leader must identify with the team's core values and motivations and draw on the energy associated with the team members' desire to drive change. The leader must create an environment in which calculated risks can be undertaken in a controlled manner.

# Am I lacking as a leader?

Are you worried that you don't have some or all of the characteristics listed above? Don't panic! The good news is that you probably *do* have at least some of these competencies – however, you must be *demonstrating* the skills you do have.

If you are feeling weak in the leadership competencies, if you're not sure whether you are demonstrating that you are a manager or a leader, there are solutions available:

1 You can recruit someone onto the team who does have the characteristics and skills that you feel you lack. In this instance, you can learn from them and they can gently remind you of the need to take the appropriate relevant action. Alternatively, you can buy in the competency. For example, if you feel setting a vision is not your strong point, you could bring in a consultant or coach who will work with you and the team to set the vision and put in place a framework to track progress.

2 You can delegate responsibility to an individual on the team, or the team as a whole. In this instance, you facilitate the environment for the skills to be developed without you having to be the focal point. For example, if creativity is not your strong point, you can ensure that you create the space for the team to brainstorm and be creative.

3 You can ask a peer, mentor or coach to keep you honest and give you tips and tricks that will help you overcome your competency deficit. This can be a very good way of making sure you maximize the coaching or mentoring relationship.

## Tips, tricks and takeaways

- **Check yourself:** Are you a leader due to the power or authority bestowed on you by someone else, or are you a leader because you have inspired others to follow you? A quick test here is to ask yourself the question, 'Why would anyone want to be led by me?'

- **Share the glory:** success can feed a competitive streak in some leaders (especially in the corporate world), but it is essential that you make sure your team is getting due credit for the success. Good leaders know that they have strengths but that they cannot succeed in the long run without relying on others. A truly confident leader is happy to share the plaudits with team members and others who provided help along the way.

- **Seek diversity in hiring:** hire people who believe what you believe, as well as those whose values are aligned to the values of your organization and are driven to live by their values. However, also make sure you include people who will bring a different perspective or point of view to the table. Diversity in all forms is essential in all high-performing teams.

- **Shake up the routine:** it is good to have a disciplined process and way of working, as that provides predictability and clarity for the other team members on what is expected. However, when things are too predictable they can run the risk of stagnating, and losing efficiency (for example, if people become bored with repetitive tasks). If you are working on a long-term initiative it may not be a bad thing to introduce a change to the routine. This can be done by swapping people's responsibilities or positions on the team, or by changing how team meetings are managed. For example, you could introduce a scenario where every fourth team meeting has no agenda and people simply talk about what is on their mind (including non-work issues).

- **Have metrics:** the old adage is true: if it is not measured it will not happen. As a leader you need to be able to objectively illustrate progress towards the goal. You need to be very clear with your team and stakeholders as to what success looks like. How will it be measured? Both hard and soft measures are needed, and the metrics *must* be available for all of the team to see.

### Reflective exercise

Undertake a 360-degree survey to get feedback from employees, peers and stakeholders. Having received the feedback, go through it with a coach or mentor and put together a development plan that will enable you to continue to leverage your strengths and address any change that you would like to make.

# PART TWO
# Managing others

# 14
# How to disagree

It is inevitable but healthy for there to be a certain level of disagreement and friction in a business. In fact, a lack of disagreement can indicate that there is either 'group think' going on, or not enough diversity of thought within the team; it may also be a symptom of the presence of an autocratic leader. For a business to function and grow, there needs to be an element of constructive disagreement within and between teams.

When presenting a counterpoint, it is important to be very specific on what it is you disagree with and not to be personal in your argument. Ensure that you present your alternative idea as an option to be considered, as opposed to a criticism. Try to find an objective way of presenting the options. Show that you understand the other person's point of view, not just by stating 'I understand your point of view' but by demonstrating that you have considered their perspective – including whether they have more authority than you, or feel more ownership over the topic being discussed. Then be specific on what elements of their point of view you can build upon, before outlining where you disagree. For instance, is there an opportunity to start the sentence with 'Yes *and*…'? The positive intent will help people understand that you are trying to be supportive and constructive, and work collaboratively, but also bring a new perspective to the table.

Commonly, disagreements stem from the following areas:

- lack of alignment on (or understanding of) the critical success factors or priorities for the business;
- utilization of finite resources, usually apparent in budget or resource allocation discussions;
- an individual's risk tolerance or perception of a likely risk;
- the perceived impact of the risk on the individual or business should the risk come to pass;
- individuals or groups with mutually exclusive goals.

# The *what* and the *how*

In any disagreement there is the 'what' and the 'how'.

## *The* what

The 'what' involves understanding the outcome or purpose of the other person's perspective and which aspect of this you disagree with. Here are some guidelines to help you solidify your position:

- Why do you disagree? Be clear and concise with no more than three to four reasons. If you have a 'laundry list' of reasons, people will think you don't have a good argument, so you are 'dredging the bottom of the barrel' to come up with objections.
- Do you fully understand the other person's perspective?
  - Are there any underlying anxieties, hopes or fears that may be influencing the other person's perspective?
  - Put yourself in their shoes: try to argue in favour of their position.
  - What anxieties, hopes or fears are underlying your opinion?
  - Is this ultimately your decision, their decision or someone senior to both of you?
- Have you or the business created an objective evaluation matrix to assess all options?

If your reason for disagreeing is subjective or emotive, don't hide it – it's OK to make people aware that you know you are acting upon your feelings. However, never present your subjective views as facts or objective data.

## *The* how

When disagreeing with the other person, it is important to ask yourself, 'How am I going to make them feel?' The purpose of the discussion is to reach a positive outcome for the business. The 'how' looks at how to present your perspective:

- Check your reasoning and rationale with a third party.
- Solicit support for your perspective. Identify an individual whose opinion is respected by the person you disagree with, then see if they can help to influence on your behalf.

- Find out if there is agreement on what success looks like at a macro level – do you agree on the main goal, and disagree only on how to get there, for example?

- Choose a good time to disagree – avoid open or public disagreement if possible, so that people don't feel put on the spot or embarrassed.

- Don't attack the other person or their views. If you can, make the person feel good about their idea or position and, if appropriate, thank them for their initiative and the thought they have put into their proposal.

- Ask the other person if they want to hear your opinion. Present your proposal as an opinion (an opinion cannot be right or wrong) and focus on presenting the positives of your view or proposal. Bring a suggested solution.

- Can you include aspects of their perspective in your proposal? Where do the two proposals complement each other? Be open to seeing the best of both worlds.

- Acknowledge the reality – ultimately, there is usually someone above you who may well have the final call (and maybe this is the person you're disagreeing with), so in most circumstances, it's appropriate to acknowledge that fact and make it clear that you will support the final decision whichever way it goes.

Always remain calm and do not take the conversation personally. In the end, any disagreements should always lead to a rational business discussion. Avoid judgemental language that could be perceived to be critical of the other person or their idea.

---

## Tips, tricks and takeaways

- **Be kind:** it is said that most people will forget what you say, most people will forget what you do but nobody ever forgets how you make them feel. It is important that if you are disagreeing with someone you do it in a manner that will not impinge upon their self-worth or dignity.

- **Be solution-oriented:** as part of your disagreement try to bring a solution or accommodation to the conversation. Some people bring a challenge but do not bring a solution to the discussion; if you only bring a challenge you are at risk of being perceived as a blocker. Be sure to maintain focus on the ultimate goal and bring a suggestion that may help address the core issues.

### Reflective exercise

Think about the last time you had a significant disagreement with someone at work. Who was it, and what was it about? How was it resolved? Is there anything you might do differently now, in order to get a different or better outcome?

# 15
# How to handle a difficult boss or peer

From time to time we will all encounter individuals who are challenging to deal with in a professional environment. While you can't control how other people behave, there are some actions you can take to address difficult situations, and navigate interactions diplomatically.

## Try not to take it personally

If an individual's conduct is having a negative effect on you, try not to take it personally. Chances are the individual developed the behaviour long before they met you and, as such, they are reacting to something that is nothing to do with you. There can be a number of factors to why some people act negatively in professional situations. Their behaviour could be pre-existing, they might not be aware of how they are coming across or they simply might not be considering the effect they are having on their colleagues. While none of these should be used as an excuse, it is important to be aware of these factors in the first instance before taking their behaviour to heart.

## Define the behaviour

What specific behaviour causes you concern? Is there more than one, or a pattern? What is the impact of that behaviour or pattern on you? When you are defining the behaviour be sure to include tone, context, and culture as well as language in your summation. The tone and context in something that is said or done can be very relevant; be sure to look at the behaviour as a whole, not just isolated words or actions. It is also good to see if the behaviour or language is used by the individual in other settings.

The next filter to apply is culture; there are behaviours that are considered perfectly normal in some cultures that would not be tolerated elsewhere. Ask yourself if the individual is acting according to their culture, or whether you are applying your own cultural lens to your interpretation of the situation. Just because something is permissible in one specific culture does not necessarily make it appropriate behaviour, but it may explain why someone is persisting with a problematic way of behaving.

# Be aware of the cause and effect

Does the individual consistently behave in this manner, or are there triggers (eg deadlines, personal stress, etc) that cause the individual to change their conduct? It is not unusual for people to behave differently depending upon the situation. For example, when someone is calm and feels in control of their situation, they may behave in an entirely appropriate fashion. However, if for some reason they feel under pressure, stressed or anxious, their behaviour may change and become 'difficult'. Pay attention to social contexts, too – if someone has been drinking, for example, would this explain the unusual behaviour?

# Don't fight fire with fire

Remain calm, don't mirror or mimic the undesirable behaviour – retain your poise and professionalism. If you need to remove yourself from the situation, excuse yourself if possible, and find somewhere to reflect and gather your thoughts.

# Look for balance

Nobody is perfect; we all have habits or idiosyncrasies that may jar a little with other people. It is worth making a conscious effort to see someone's more attractive behavioural traits. It may even be appropriate to encourage these traits, if you can – positive reinforcement can be a powerful interpersonal tool. In short, it is important to view the whole person, rather than focus exclusively on a micro trait or issue.

# Try to make the individual aware

Most people know how they behave each day, but not everyone is aware of the impact of their actions on others. What some people will regard as funny, others will regard as insulting, so you should try explaining the impact of the behaviour on you. Pick an appropriate time and location for a discussion – it is important that the person is in a position to be receptive to feedback. Don't attack the behaviour, as this will probably make the person feel defensive; simply make them aware of how their behaviour is affecting you – leave it to them to decide what to do next.

For example, someone who swears or tells inappropriate jokes in the office would in many contexts be considered to be displaying bad or offensive behaviour. If you were to approach them and say 'I find your swearing offensive; I wish you would stop', you are being critical of their behaviour and will probably provoke a defensive, negative reaction. However, if you say 'When you swear, I feel uncomfortable; are you aware of how aggressive you sound?', you may get a much more reasoned response. In the second instance, you are not criticizing the behaviour, you are simply making the person aware of the impact they are having on you and leaving it up to them how to respond.

# Act early

Many people are tempted to put up with a situation rather than address it – either because they feel awkward, or they don't know how. Frequently, it's minor issues that have accumulated over time that cause problems, rather than one major incident, so it is preferable to act immediately if you feel uncomfortable with someone's behaviour, even if they have not crossed a major line. It is very difficult for someone to make an immediate change if discussions begin with 'Two months ago...'. If the behaviour occurred previously and you took no action at the time, then there is a possibility your silence could be viewed by the individual as tacit acceptance of the behaviour – so try to act early rather than letting problems build.

# Draw a line in the sand

Eventually, if a certain behaviour continues to be a problem, you will have to make a decision. When you sense that it might be reaching this point, be sure to make a record of the issues, and use this information to determine when it is necessary to raise the issue formally. If you have taken action to address the behaviour but have not seen a change, it may be time to involve HR or the appropriate third party. It is important not to let yourself become a victim of someone else's behaviour if you feel the situation is not going to change, so you need to allow the correct channels time to attempt to resolve the issue. If this final step doesn't work – if the organization is prepared to tolerate the negative behaviour – then it may be worth considering whether the organization is one you want to be involved with.

# Due diligence

If you are about to raise an issue it is important to have done your due diligence, so that you have a cogent, well-formulated perspective in advance of approaching the problem person, or a third party. Ask yourself these questions:

- Are there cultural norms or generally accepted customs and practice that may be prevailing – ie is the conduct you are witnessing isolated to one individual, or is it endemic within the group or company?

- Is there anything that you are doing or not doing that may indicate to others that you approve of or at least accept their actions?

- Are you modelling appropriate behaviours?

- Is the behaviour that you are witnessing sporadic or consistent? Is there an underlying anxiety or stress that may be leading to the difficult behaviour?

- Are you being reasonable – would most people find this behaviour difficult, or could it be something that gets to you in particular?

- Have you checked your own thinking for any unconscious bias that may be influencing your judgement?

## Tips, tricks and takeaways

- **Sounding board:** in a situation that is impacting you on a personal level, it is advisable to engage with a trusted confidant who can act as a sounding board. (This should be someone who can provide an objective perspective. If that's someone outside of work, try to choose someone who understands the cultural norms of your industry. Be more careful if choosing a colleague or peer; they may be constrained by company policies or have to work with the difficult person themselves, and so may not be able to be objective or informal.) The process of explaining the situation to a third party is cathartic in and of itself, and may help you see something in the situation that you had not seen before. Encourage this person to challenge your perceptions of the behaviour, and to validate whether your response is reasonable.

- **Feelings:** a feeling is never right or wrong; it is simply a result of encountering a positive or negative stimulus. When dealing with difficult behaviour, it is always important to explain the situation in the context of how you feel. The objective is to make the individual aware of their impact on you.

## Reflective exercise

Think about the last time someone really irritated or frightened you, or otherwise got under your skin. How did you handle it?

- Did you ignore it, or address the behaviour?

- Did you check in with your own reactions and potential biases, or react instinctively?

- Thinking about the tips above, is there anything you would have handled differently?

# 16
# Leading teams

Your primary responsibility as the leader of a team is to enable the team members to deliver an impact that is more than just the sum of the parts. The leader is core to the creation of a motivational environment – are team members getting energy and inspiration from each other, and from their involvement in the team?

## How to be an effective team leader

Individuals on the team will look to the leader to provide many things, but the recurring themes tend to centre on the following: a successful leader will be authentic, provide significance or a sense of purpose, be excited and elicit excitement, and engender a sense of community or belonging and trust within the team. Ultimately, as the leader your role is to inspire additional discretionary effort from individuals for the benefit of the organization and the team.

As the leader of a team you must ask yourself the following:

- Is everyone clear on the team's purpose?
- Is everyone clear on what is expected from them and each other?
- Have I created an environment in which the team can individually and collectively do their best work?

While these may seem like simple questions, all too often the root cause of frustration for teams is a lack of clarity on what success looks like. Ultimately, this can be a key factor in the success or failure of the team, so it is critical for the leader to provide this clarity and continually reinforce the collective priorities. This is perhaps even more important in organizations with a flat structure – traditional, 'ladder-based' career progression may be slower in this kind of culture, meaning that individuals will need to look for meaning, or a sense of achievement or recognition, from sources other than traditional promotions, including feeling a valuable part of the team they are on.

- Does everyone on the team feel accountable for the collective success or failure of the team?

- Do any members of the team feel more affinity to another team?

Some teams are formed simply because the individuals all happen to report to the same boss, as opposed to being brought together to deliver on a common purpose. Consequently, individuals may feel more affinity to another group within the company. This is not necessarily a bad thing, but it does need to be understood. The leader of the team needs to take this into consideration when managing employees.

- Is the team balanced? Do you have a diverse set of skills and experience on the team?

- What is the working dynamic for conflict resolution? Is there a high level of trust?

- How well does the team know stakeholder needs, and are these needs different from the success factors of the team?

- How will you ensure that the team sustains high performance as individuals leave or join the team? (For more, see Chapter 33 on succession planning.)

## Have you got the right team culture?

It is important to establish the culture for the team and ensure that the culture is maintained as the composition of the team changes over time:

- Have you made it easy for people to challenge you and others on the team?

- Do the team members feel comfortable bringing bad news to the team? If there is a blame culture, it is likely people will avoid bringing up bad news, which may prevent the team dealing efficiently with issues.

- Are you providing appropriate recognition? This is vitally important: successful leaders understand the motivational power of giving appropriate recognition to team members. A simple 'thank you' or expression of appreciation can be very energizing, and a strong leader will provide both public and private recognition on a regular basis.

- Have you set enough time aside for innovative creative thinking? Do you foster and incubate ideas?

# Tough conversations

From time to time you will have to have a tough conversation with a team member. Take inspiration from the following approach:

- **Be strong and curious:** people tend to prefer a leader who presents a fact-based, cogent perspective, rather than one who tries to please everyone. Start from the position of trying to gain a complete understanding of what is behind the problem; what are the underlying anxieties, fears or issues that may be influencing the person concerned?

- **Listen:** in a tough conversation, it is better to do more listening than talking. Sometimes, simply the act of listening with an open mind will convey a level of respect for the other person; they will feel that they have been heard, and that they had the opportunity to express their views.

- **Be direct:** get to the point of the conversation quickly, and express clearly what outcome you would like to see as a result of the conversation. Don't sugar-coat the message; acknowledge the issue and explain your perspective.

- **Be decisive:** it is much better to address a conflict as early as possible. People may not like negative feedback but in the long run they will respect it, and you for having the courage to give it.

- **Focus on a positive outcome:** focus on getting to a successful conclusion; don't wallow in worry before the conversation. Most people want to reach agreement, so it is important to keep the bigger picture in mind and search for areas of common ground from which you can build for a successful outcome.

# Delegation

The key to good quality delegation is to make it very clear up front how and when you want to be involved in the decision-making process. You must first challenge yourself on how much control you want or need to have: if you find yourself believing that you need to be involved in every aspect of decision making, this could be indicative of a lack of trust in your team, or an inability as a leader to delegate effectively. Above all, when it comes to delegating, it is imperative that you are very clear on your expectations, on the level of involvement you want, and how and when you want to be communicated to over time.

There are typically five levels of delegation. See Table 16.1 below:

**Table 16.1**   Levels of delegation

| Level | Description | Manager's involvement |
|---|---|---|
| 1 | You empower the individual to do research, but you retain the responsibility to come up with a recommendation and all decision-making authority. | 100% |
| 2 | You empower the individual to do research and make a recommendation, but you retain approval and decision-making authority. | 85% |
| 3 | You empower the individual to do research and make the decision, but not to act upon the decision without your prior approval. | 70% |
| 4 | You empower the individual to do research, make and implement the decision without your prior approval, and just inform you when the action is taken. | 10% |
| 5 | You empower the individual to do research, make and implement the decision without your prior approval or involvement in any aspect of the process. | 0% |

## Tips, tricks and takeaways

- **Situation:** leadership is situational, so check that you are applying different approaches in differing situations. Teams can and should have leadership at all levels, so it is appropriate for you to give responsibility for leading certain events or aspects of the business to others on the team.

- **Be consistent and predictable:** a leader's actions and words must be consistent. An erratic or inconsistent leader will only serve to create ambiguity, which may induce people to leave the team.

- **Refresh:** ensure that you schedule off-site time for the team to bond. All teams need to take stock and self-assess their own way of working. It is important to prevent the team from just drifting along. As the leader, you need to formally close completed assignments, recognize accomplishments and prioritize.

- **Discipline:** it is important to review progress in a disciplined manner on a monthly basis and review performance metrics. These should not be casual meetings, but an in-depth performance analysis to see if you are on track from a strategic perspective. These meetings provide the early-warning signs that you are on- or off-track, so you must challenge to ensure that people are not telling you what you want to hear.

## Reflective exercise

Go back through your work activities for the last day/week/month – you can check emails, to-do lists, etc, to help you remember:

- How many of these tasks were delegated?
- How many could have been delegated, but weren't?
- How many were delegated, but perhaps shouldn't have been?

# 17
# Supporting a team's work–life balance

High-performing companies recognize that their long-term sustained success is attributable to the motivation of their people, and a key part of determining whether or not your employees are capable of sustaining high performance is determined by whether or not they can maintain a reasonable work–life balance. Managing work–life balance appropriately should be a key element of your company's HR strategy, then – because enabling a healthy work–life balance is key to attracting talent and motivating and enabling people (ie ensuring that your staff both *want* to, and are *able* to give their best in the long term).

Both work and life will throw up disruptions and seemingly conflicting priorities, so each individual must be equipped with the wherewithal to manage the balance in their own life, and as a manager and leader you are well positioned to support this.

## What makes a good work–life balance?

Healthy work–life balance is all about behaviour, actions and habits. As a leader, here are some helpful actions for you to support others:

- Talk about what constitutes a good work–life balance for each person and have periodic reviews of how their situation is working for them.

- Provide clarity on the company's expectations of the individual to minimize ambiguity. This includes having clear policies for remote working, core hours, use of technology, etc, and ensuring that these policies are implemented consistently. Many companies have clear policies, but in allowing 'manager discretion' inadvertently create inconsistency in the implementation. Some roles by their very nature do not lend themselves to flexible work practices, and most employees will understand the rationale for such scenarios, but it is important to be clear on policy exceptions.

- If possible, allow people control over their own schedule.
- Recognize the peaks and troughs in demands upon an individual's schedule.
- Consistency is critical – while you are trying to give people flexibility, this cannot be unrestrained, as it then has the potential to cause issues for others on the team.

The challenge of addressing the work–life balance within a team is that there are a variety of individual circumstances. It helps to think of it as a state that needs to be nurtured and re-evaluated consistently. For example, individuals may be OK with making a personal sacrifice to achieve a goal as long as they feel that they are managing and prioritizing their own time – because that way, it is their choice – so the solution is not necessarily to re-move the challenge, but to allow people to be in control of their own work as much as possible.

The single biggest feature of a positive work–life balance is the feeling of control. Most people are energized by taking on challenging opportunities, so if they are allowed to take ownership of achieving a good outcome, they are more likely to feel good about their work–life balance.

The big threats to work–life balance are inconsistency, ambiguity and a lack of support from team or family members. As we plan our schedules, we all need an element of consistency. Some aspects of the weeks and months need to be predictable – especially those aspects that pertain to our physical and mental health. Adequate sleep, exercise and 'me time' need to be planned into the schedule as non-negotiables, and as a leader you need to allow your team the space to be able to take advantage of this.

## *Provide clarity to reduce ambiguity*

As a leader, you have a key role in ensuring that there is no ambiguity of expectation when it comes to work deliverables. Not understanding what is expected of them can be a source of stress for many people, so being very clear in setting expectations for the outputs you expect from your team will help them plan. Lack of clarity at the outset will inevitably lead to disap-pointment and the need for a last-minute scramble, which will then impact work–life balance. Therefore, when taking on something new, begin with the end in mind – make sure you calibrate with other stakeholders on the specifics of the expectations and outcomes. It's no good having clear policies and a high level of flexibility if the work itself is not clearly planned and communicated – being constantly in 'fire-fighting' mode won't allow people to make the best use of wellbeing policies.

# Consistency is critical

As mentioned above, consistency is important for a number of reasons – from making sure that people don't feel that some managers are 'fairer' than others, to making sure that one person's need for time doesn't impact another person's need for a manageable workload. One way to approach this balance of flexibility and consistency is to set the parameters within which people can be flexible – for example, it is perfectly reasonable for you to have core hours, or a rule that all internal meetings take place between 10 am and 4 pm.

Most people will understand when they join a company that they will probably have to make some compromises or adjustments to fit in with the company culture and work schedule. It would be unusual for anybody to expect to have complete control over their workload – the key is to communicate clearly what the business needs are, so that people understand where there might be room for flexibility, and where there isn't.

# How does your work–life balance affect others?

It is not unusual for a manager or leader to have a reasonable work–life balance, but unwittingly have an impact on the work–life balance of their team. For example, a manager who sends work emails while they are waiting to pick up their children from extra-curricular activities in the evening (harmless on the surface), may unthinkingly make their team feel as if they should also be keeping up with emails outside of work hours.

Managers and leaders should be cognizant, therefore, that their behaviour will set a tone for the organization or team. Many team members will consciously or subconsciously feel they have to mirror the behaviour of the manager or leader (eg hours spent in the office, emails sent after hours). Many managers will talk very positively about the importance of work–life balance but then spend enormous amounts of time in the office or working remotely – in this scenario, actions speak louder than words. Instead, leaders should be *seen* to take holidays, leave the office early on occasion, take time off for medical appointments, and keep family or personal commitments such as volunteering or attending parent–teacher conferences. These actions will demonstrate to others that it is acceptable and encouraged to manage their own work–life balance.

## Tips, tricks and takeaways

- **Not just time:** be aware that work–life balance is not always a time issue. Sometimes people will be in control of their time, but find that work impacts their life outside of normal work hours, for example they can't relax properly outside of work because they are always thinking about work-related issues.

- **Be a role model:** the impact of what you say about work–life balance will be reinforced or diminished by your actions. It is very important as a leader that you role-model a good work–life balance. This may mean deliberately leaving the office early on one or two evenings a week.

## Reflective exercise

Assess what impact your own work–life balance is having on your team members, whether they are direct reports or peers:

- Do you work remotely, or have flexible hours? What do team members do when you are not here – is the process clear?

- Do you ever send emails after hours or very early in the morning?

- Are you often the first to arrive *and* the last to leave?

- Do you use your annual leave? Do people know when you do?

- Do you go to the doctor or dentist promptly when you need to, even if it means taking time off work? Do people know when you have to do this?

- Do you take a sick day when you're ill, or are you known for coming into work even when you're headachy, coughing and sneezing?

- Do you do work when you're on holiday?

# 18

# Performance discussions (as a manager)

The purpose of a good quality performance discussion is to recognize the individual appropriately for their work, motivate them to continue to produce good work, and help them to learn and develop professionally. As a manager or leader, it is your responsibility to develop talent in the organization, and the performance discussion – or appraisal, or review, or one-to-one – should be seen as a talent development enabling process rather than simply a progress review.

Research indicates that it is not simply having high performers that matters, but ensuring you are using your high-performing talent on the most important strategic initiatives that will bring long-term benefit to the organization.

## Deliver positive results in performance discussions

When you are meeting with direct reports for a performance discussion or review, you will be looking for the discussion to have a positive result. These outcomes include:

- The individual feels appropriately recognized for their contribution.
- The individual feels listened to in terms of ideas they may have for their own development.
- The individual feels motivated and excited about their future and the team/company's future.
- The individual understands the feedback and the relevance of the feedback in the context of their development and their role.

- The individual clearly understands their development areas, feels ownership for the actions and is motivated to address those development needs.

- The individual feels that they have their boss's support in pursuing a development plan.

To achieve the outcomes above, the feedback must be extremely clear, relevant and supported by objective data. Great feedback is focused on the future; it will encourage the individual to continue to grow and develop.

After the meeting, keep an eye out for evidence of the individual responding to the feedback. If you notice positive changes in approach or behaviour, be sure to recognize those changes swiftly and offer encouragement.

# Performance discussions with a high-performing individual

In addition to the outcomes listed above, you will need to add a further dimension to this review. If you have a high-performing employee, you can be sure that others (both internally and externally) will have noticed this individual's performance and you could run the risk of losing the employee to a competitor.

The performance discussion is therefore a chance to 're-recruit' the individual. You could almost think of them as someone you are trying to poach from another company; make the conversation about them, and what you can do to help them achieve their goals and develop their career.

It is important to challenge yourself as follows:

- Are we using this high-performing individual in the best way for the company's long-term success?

- Are they in a business-critical role? If not, you probably need to move the individual into a more important role.

# Performance discussions with a low-performing individual

Remember, your company hired the individual for their demonstrable skill at some point, so to some extent you are accountable for the situation that now exists. The content of the discussion should never be a surprise to the individual, as you should have been giving feedback in the moment as you witnessed good or substandard performance. The objective of the discussion is to identify a positive outcome for both the company and the individual, bearing in mind that the outcome may mean that the individual leaves the company. It is important to be well prepared for the discussion with the low-performing employee, and be sure to ask yourself the following questions in advance of the discussion:

- What specifically is the individual lacking to be successful in the role? Are the answers to this question objective or subjective? Do you have feedback from third parties to support your view?

- Is the individual talented, but in the wrong job?

- Is the dip in performance temporary or prolonged? Is the individual temporarily distracted by non-work factors, eg a sick relative, relationship issues or financial pressure?

- Would the individual have been more successful if they had received more support from you or others in the company?

You have the opportunity to help the individual use the opportunity wisely and constructively. Because of this, in the meeting you need to adhere to the following:

- **Be very factual:** focus the conversation on *controllable* deliverables and outcomes. Remember the individual's dignity, and do not make the conversation a personal attack. If an individual fails to deliver due to an uncontrollable event, then the feedback can focus on the individual's reaction to that event and whether or not it is reasonable to expect that they should have had a viable contingency in place.

- **Be balanced:** inevitably, the individual will have some strengths – recognize those strengths but do not obscure the primary message. Sugar-coating the message may confuse the individual or, worse still, they may not get the key points you were trying to make. Therefore, separate the two aspects of the feedback: give the positive feedback and then address the less positive feedback.

- **Be very clear on next steps:** put a plan in place and make it as objective as possible with clear deliverables and timelines. Make it clear what the consequences of not meeting the requirements of the plan will be.

- **Listen with an open mind:** you need to give the individual the opportunity to express themselves. By listening with an open mind, you will get a better understanding of how you can help the employee address the situation. It will also help you understand the employee's perspective – you may learn something that changes how you approach the next steps.

- **Write down your feedback:** sometimes employers tend not to follow up a clear conversation with a written summary of the key points of the discussion. All important points must be put in writing and sent to the employee in a timely fashion. Points made verbally in the meeting cannot be used in the event that the employee subsequently ends up in dispute with the company. Only written feedback is admissible in any formal dispute resolution process, unless you have recorded the conversation. However, before recording a conversation you must get the employee's consent to both the act of recording the conversation *and* how you intend to use the recording.

- **Giving feedback:** the content of a performance review meeting should never be a complete surprise, so it's important to check that you have been providing feedback (both positive and formative, in writing and more informally) to the individual over the last few weeks or months. In the case of a low performer, verbal feedback alone can quite often be ineffectual, and – in a worst-case scenario – it is often not admissible in a disciplinary procedure. Don't forget, too, that high performers need to get recognition – it is the fuel that will keep them motivated.

  Are you very clear on the message you want to deliver in the meeting? In the case of a high performer, be sure not to over promise or give the impression that you can enable a future benefit that is not within your sphere of influence. In the case of a low performer it is important that your message is balanced but check to ensure that the core message has been properly understood by the individual. Sugar coating the message can lead to the individual misunderstanding the pertinent points.

---

## Tips, tricks and takeaways

- **Be kind and clear:** in the case of a low performer, you want the person to remember the conversation as being a key part of their personal development; it should not in any way come across as a personal attack or impinge upon their dignity or self-worth. A good outcome would be that they understand what it is they have to do and understand the consequences of not meeting the requirements, as well as knowing that you are willing to help them if they are willing to help themselves.

## Reflective exercise

Practise an imaginary performance review with a colleague or peer and get feedback from them on the language you are using. Specifically, get your colleague to check for the clarity of your message and the balance in your approach: nobody is perfect, so there must be development needs to be discussed, and there must be a few positive attributes that the person displays, so these must be recognized too.

Alternatively, you could practise for a real performance review you have to give – but ensure that the person you practise with is appropriate. It should not be a colleague who knows the person, or will have to continue working with them.

# 19
# Impact and influence

As a leader, your effectiveness is largely dependent upon your impact and your ability to influence others to support your vision, or support you to achieve your desired goals.

The focus of this chapter is to help you orient your thoughts as you prepare for critical meetings with management or key clients, in two forms:

1 Getting the right result in a meeting with a senior executive or client.

2 Making an impact when you are *not* the subject matter expert.

## Meeting with a senior executive or key client

The key is always preparation and groundwork prior to the engagement or meeting.

### Before the meeting

Prior to engaging with the person you want to impress, you need to have done your groundwork by answering the questions below:

1 **Why is your topic important?** Both to you, and to the management/client you are trying to influence? Aim to be able to explain the importance of the topic to a third party in plain English in 90 seconds – if it's not clear or it takes longer than that, then you need to sharpen your message.

2 **What is the outcome you want to achieve?** Be specific on what success looks like for the discussion – what outcome are you hoping for? Express your answer as a definitive action, agreement to proceed or decision. Is there any outcome that you want to avoid at all costs? You should be able to summarize your answer in no more than three or four prioritized bullet points. If you find you have a 'laundry list' of desired outcomes, then you need to prioritize.

**3 What impression do you want to make?** Do you want to leave the impression that you are a subject matter expert or a leader? Subject matter experts tend to love talking about the detail; leaders tend to talk about the salient points and stay focused on the purpose of the discussion rather than the detail.

**4 What is your style?** What format is the meeting going to take, a presentation or a discussion? I tend to think 'engagement' via discussion is the answer – a presentation tends to be a one-way, one-off broadcast, whereas engagement implies a dialogue, which can be sustained over time and tends to have a greater, longer-term impact.

**5 Who are the influencers?** Whose opinion does management/the client value? Who do they listen to? Can you brief the influencers in advance? This point is critical: sometimes you have overcome more than half the battle if you can get the manager/client's trusted confidant to support your point of view. It is well worth investing time and energy in identifying the influencers and working with them in advance of the actual meeting or engagement. In fact, if you do this well, you may find you have achieved your outcome before the meeting even starts.

**6 Who are the decision makers?** Why are they the decision makers? What do they value? What expertise do they bring to the decision? Stakeholder identification is important. It is also important to understand whether they are supportive, neutral or detractors of your point of view.

**7 Identify the environment and language:** What is going on elsewhere in the business that will distract management/the client from your message? Can this be leveraged for your benefit? What is their preferred style and language? For example, sales and marketing may tend to find operations dull, so engage them by talking about how your idea will help them increase revenue/margin/market share or brand awareness. On the other hand, if you are talking to finance you may choose to highlight process controls, risk mitigation and so on.

**8 What is the physical plan?** Where are you on the agenda? Should you sit or stand? Will all key stakeholders be physically present or dialling in from a remote location?

**9 Organize your pre-meeting actions:**

   **a** Talk to the influencers and decision makers to solicit support for your position.

   **b** Talk to the chief of staff or PA to get answers to the questions above.

    **c** Have two versions of your topic prepared – the three-minute version and the 10-minute version.

    **d** Is the timing right for the meeting – should the meeting go ahead?

## During the meeting

**1 Acknowledge the reality and be a priority:** if your topic is a low priority to the audience, empathize with them, but educate them on why they need to care. One way to do this is to present your topic to management or the client in the context of one of *their* top priorities.

**2 Recognize the audience knowledge imbalance:** make a decision – do I need to educate or ignore those who are not up to speed? If you decide to bring everyone up to the same level of understanding on the topic, be sure to explain to the group what you are doing so that those who are knowledgeable don't feel you are patronizing them or wasting their time. If you decide it is not necessary to bring everyone up to speed during the meeting, be sure to offer to explain more after the meeting to those who are not knowledgeable on the topic.

**3 Be concise and deliberate:** never use more than three or four points to carry your argument. More than this implies that you don't think any of the points are strong enough to carry the argument on their own merit.

**4 Act like a leader:** if you want to be perceived as a leader, act like a leader – sit in a prominent position and make your presence felt by asking insightful questions or making helpful suggestions. You can also inspire confidence and trust by being constructive. Think about how you can build upon the points raised by others, rather than criticizing their perspective.

**5 Listen! Don't just broadcast:** people frequently get so caught up in their own message that they don't listen to what others are saying – be sure to 'listen to understand' as opposed to 'listening to respond'. Listening to understand is listening to the other person in a manner that allows you to comprehend not only what they are saying, but also the underlying anxiety that may be inherent in their point of view. Essentially, you are listening so that you can build upon their perspective and incorporate their hopes or fears in your view or at least mitigate their concerns so that they feel heard. Many people fall into the trap of 'broadcasting' and as such fail to pick up on the verbal and non-verbal signals. To have an impact there must be an *engagement* with the key individuals. A good engagement will by its very nature be a two-way dialogue, so demonstrate that you are open minded and not simply stuck 'on message'.

**6 Pay attention:** listen to the question and answer what you have been asked, not what you think you should have been asked.

## After the meeting

Make sure you take a meaningful action from the meeting and execute it within a specific time period. Taking an action gives you the opportunity to continue the engagement, as opposed to simply making an impression in the meeting but then being forgotten about afterwards. If you do not have a specific action, it is good practice to summarize the result of the discussion in an email to double-check that everyone is aligned.

# Make an impact when you are not the subject matter expert

Sometimes you will find yourself in a situation where you have to lead a team of experts or work with people who have far more knowledge and experience than you – don't let this intimidate you, as your lack of knowledge may help others to think differently about the topic. For example, in having to explain to you the context and argument for their point of view, the subject matter expert (SME) may uncover a flaw in their logic or perspective.

Knowledge is a wonderful commodity, but it is only relevant if it is used to generate a business insight. Knowledge can sometimes paralyse or induce fear (of failure, for example), so your lack of knowledge can actually be an asset.

If you are not the SME, you will need to bring the following attributes to the meeting:

- **Fresh thinking and no baggage:** as a non-SME, you bring a different mindset. Without a position to defend, you are free to have an open mind and bring a fresh perspective.

- **No ego:** many people have a passionate association with the status quo, largely because they may have created it, feel associated with it or have become comfortable with it. As a result, they may perceive a change to the status quo as an implied criticism. Your lack of ego should enable you to be constructive and orient the conversation to be forward looking.

- **Leadership:** a strong leader helps bring clarity, structure, resilience and energy to the discussion. You can do all of the above without being an SME. You can also help to tease out other points of view.

- **Critical and insightful thinking:** as a non-SME you can ask very basic questions and you probably won't make assumptions to the same extent as an SME. The quality of your questions can be invaluable in helping to bring clarity to the discussion.

- **Support for SMEs:** all experts need support to bring their ideas forward or to turn an idea into action. Your enthusiasm and support can help create the momentum to get the idea off the ground.

- **No fear:** your lack of knowledge may mean you bring a degree of confidence or conviction to the situation that may become infectious to the team. Remember knowledge can be an inhibitor, especially if it induces fear in individuals.

---

## Tips, tricks and takeaways

- **Focus on what is important to the other person:** remember what is important to you may not be important to management/the client – they pay you to worry about the detail, so don't fall into the trap of pulling them into the detail unless it is completely necessary. Always focus on what is important to the manager/client and illustrate how the topic will enable them to be successful or achieve their goals.

- **Give support and recognition:** set yourself up as someone who can support the SMEs, ie someone who recognizes, values and appreciates their knowledge. If you are the leader, always give due recognition to the source of the knowledge or expertise when presenting the decision.

- **Get another point of view:** if you can, try to solicit a perspective from others who have dealt with your audience in advance of the meeting – they may be able to give you helpful insights.

## Reflective exercise

Before the engagement ask yourself:

- What is unique about me or my approach that will elicit the desired outcome?
- What have I learnt from previous important meetings that I could carry into this engagement?

After the engagement with the manager or client, pause and ask yourself three questions:

1 What worked well?

2 What should I do more of?

3 What should I do differently to obtain a different outcome?

# 20
# Challenging the status quo

Solving short-term problems keeps people busy and usually results in immediate gratification or recognition when an issue is resolved. It is natural to focus on the short-term issues largely because they are within one's control, they are usually obvious and most importantly they will have the most immediate impact. The satisfaction arising from the completion of a short-term task becomes the drug that fuels continued focus on the here and now.

This short-term focus inevitably gives us a convenient excuse not to plan for future opportunities. Successful leaders, though, are always thinking about what lies ahead, including anything that will have to be changed to sustain success over the long term.

## Driving change

Successful leaders recognize the need to prepare for the long term, and also to get people ready to follow them and accept any associated change. We must reward ourselves and those around us for taking a long-term view.

As a leader, when initiating change it is important to focus on the following principles:

### *Be clear and concise*

The first step to driving change is to be very clear about the vision for the future and make it compelling. What will success look and feel like for you and others? How will you know you have achieved your vision? You will need to be able to sell your vision and to help others see it with the same clarity as you. Remember, you have probably been thinking about your vision for quite a while, but others will have to go through that thinking process and will need you to make it easy for them to understand. Lack of clarity in the vision will give rise to confusion and a lack of motivation to follow you, so it is important to be able to illustrate how customers or clients will benefit, and how employees will benefit. Inherent in challenging the status quo – or driving change – is that you will take people out of their comfort zone, so there must be a compelling reason to encourage people to move.

## Prioritize your ideas

Distil your ideas down to the two or three most impactful suggestions. This eliminates confusion and allows others to focus on the core of your vision, rather than being distracted by peripheral 'nice to have' benefits. The probability is that if you can get the group to deliver on your top three ideas, the other peripheral benefits will follow fairly swiftly. If you present a 'laundry list' of priorities, then people may feel that no single priority is worthy on its own and lose interest.

## Solicit support

Acting alone may not always be the most effective way to drive change; sometimes it pays to build a groundswell of support. Solicit allies who will promote your cause, or at the very least support you at key moments. Middle managers can be key in this regard, as they have a huge impact on how the proposed change is received in the organization. It is important to involve these managers early – include them in the design of the change. Also, look for evangelists or key influencers in the team who, either by personality or general popularity, are listened to by others. If you can get these people on board with the change early, then roll-out will be much easier.

## Don't give up too soon

Many good ideas can wither on the vine – not because they weren't good ideas, but because the owner of the idea did not persist in refining and promoting it. Communicate your idea in a manner and language that resonates with the audience. Be prepared for setbacks, take a long-term view and be resilient. If you find yourself coming up against resistance, it is worth exploring the key reasons people resist change:

- Fear of the unknown or fear of failure.
- Perceived or real threat to status or job.
- Conflicting priorities – it is not simply enough to get support for your initiative; you need to get people to agree to prioritize your initiative over their current goals.
- Lack of understanding of either the reason for the change or the envisaged future state. People may understand that there is a need for a change, but they won't move until they understand that the future state is better than the current situation. This may be expressed as 'better the devil you know' or 'don't jump out of the frying pan into the fire'.

### Don't be obsessive

Always keep your mind open. Your idea might be good, but there may also be better ideas out there. Keep your perspective, but remember that it may be right to pursue another idea and then return to yours.

### Resources

Ensure you are clear about the resources required to implement and sustain the change. If a change initiative fails, it is often because the required resources were not allocated to ensuring its success. Resources will be needed for three distinct phases: the launch phase of the change (due diligence and planning); the implementation phase (including the creation of a knowledge repository); and the handover phase (the transition of the change into day-to-day business).

# Make change the focus

It is important to lead by example. The first thing those people you are asking to change will look for is evidence of you changing or doing something differently. Actions speak louder than words, so leading by example is critical. To do this, you will need to make your change very visible to others.

Be quick to recognize others who demonstrate an action or bias for the change. A salary is what an employee works for, but recognition and praise is what they thrive on. Be very public in your recognition of others, both formally with awards but also informally with simple expressions of gratitude and kindness. Sustained change has a strong correlation with the recognition you give to those making the change happen.

The key word to remember here is: reinforce. Reinforce your message! You can't communicate enough in a time of change, you must use every opportunity to reinforce the message. You must stay on message and be consistent in your communication of the vision.

## Tips, tricks and takeaways

- **Remove barriers to change:** typical barriers to change include: old systems and processes; outdated procedures; people clinging to the status quo because they are rewarded for it; fear of failure; or a combination of the above.

- **The burning platform:** it is not unusual for the team to become comfortable with the status quo. To initiate the change, you have to do two things: paint a picture that illustrates how the status quo will not be attractive in the future (the burning platform) and illustrate the benefits of the changed state.

- **Rules versus innovation:** are you rewarding people for adhering to rules, or are you rewarding them for finding innovative solutions?

- **Recognition:** in any impetus to challenge the status quo you need to be able to answer the question 'What's in it for me?' for all stakeholders and impacted parties. The question may not materialize overtly but will nonetheless be lurking in the backs of people's minds. It is very important that you illustrate how individuals will be recognized for joining you in the initiative.

- **Communication:** change is fuelled by communication. Never assume people are fully behind you or completely understand your perspective. It is imperative that you continually reiterate the importance of achieving the goals and the associated benefits. In addition, it is important to be able to illustrate what underpins your confidence in achieving the goal. This latter point is usually achieved by being able to show progress towards the goal and by being transparent about how you are mitigating risks and issues.

- **Speed is important:** change needs to happen swiftly, otherwise it becomes a slog. To generate momentum, look for short-term wins and publicize those wins. Never underestimate the power of momentum; this, combined with communication, can lead to a change initiative becoming a self-fulfilling prophesy. The momentum of the project and associated speed of implementation will be impacted by the level of visibility and recognition that is garnered from early quick wins. If the initiative requires an organization design change, then I would suggest implementing that change as early and as swiftly as possible. The more the organization's structure is aligned to the change, the greater the likelihood of the change enduring.

- **Risks and issues:** early identification of risks and issues, along with a transparent and disciplined approach to mitigating the issues, will give people confidence in the initiative. Change initiatives can be undermined when people feel that risks and issues are not being taken seriously. It is good to be transparent with risks and issues.

- **Timing:** most organizations have a relatively predictable annual cycle of operations or business planning rhythm. There are times when the senior leadership team are preoccupied with short-term challenges, and there are times when they may be more open minded to considering new ideas for change. It is important to bring forward your idea at a time when it is most likely to be positively received.

## Reflective exercise

Think about an idea you have to challenge the status quo. Who are the key stakeholders and people impacted? Make a list, as fully as you can, and categorize them under three headings:

1 Supporters of the idea.

2 Neutral.

3 Actively against your proposal.

Take time to think about why each person might be in each category.

**For supporters:** How can you make the most of their support? Do you think they are aware of what you expect from them in actively engaging and demonstrating their support? If any of them could be described as passive supporters, how could you encourage them to become active supporters?

**For those who are neutral:** What can you do to move them from being neutral to supporting the idea? How might you prevent them from slipping into being against your proposal?

**For those who are actively against your proposal:** Can you understand their concerns? If you think you already understand their concerns, how might you mitigate them? Are there any common themes or underlying anxieties for this group that would cause them to resist your change and cling to the status quo?

# 21
# Building a culture of innovation

A culture of innovation recognizes that it is imperative to create an environment of continuous learning in the workplace. People will be recognized and rewarded for taking a growth mindset approach to their daily tasks.

The culture of the group or organization is heavily influenced by the actions of its leader. A leader cannot support the development of a culture of innovation with words alone – they must be seen to actively support initiatives with appropriate investment of resources and time. The key role of the leader is to create an environment within which innovation can flourish.

## How can you encourage innovation?

First, as the leader it is important that you schedule an opportunity for your team to think creatively about the future. It is easy for focus to become centred on the immediacy of day-to-day challenges as there is invariably a need for action to be taken. As a result of this, it is important to take yourself and your team out of their usual routine to think imaginatively about how to shape the future and sow the seeds that will generate long-term benefits.

By allowing time for creative thought, you signal your intent to encourage innovation. But as the leader, you must also be public and vocal about your support by creating the right environment to facilitate innovation. This will include the following:

1 Freeing up the time and space for people to be creative.
2 Explaining the framework within which you want the innovation or creativity to operate – in other words, outlining the most pressing business challenges that require innovative or creative solutions:
   a Be clear on the criteria to evaluate success for each challenge identified.
   b Be clear on how you will prioritize ideas for piloting.

    **c**  Creativity is an iterative process, not an event.

    **d**  Creativity needs imagination, action and application.

    **e**  Innovation is the process of putting an idea into action to deliver value or solve a human need.

**3** Rewarding and recognizing those who attempt to innovate (including those initiatives that 'fail'). Ensure people recognize that not all initiatives will be a success, and that in the spirit of 'nothing ventured, nothing gained' they may take calculated risks. It is important that everyone learns from the initiatives that failed. Specifically, what could have been done differently to make the initiative a success? What prevailing assumptions were proved to be inaccurate? If the learning can be captured, future initiatives will stand a greater chance of success.

**4** Create a lab or space for piloting ideas. Pilots or tests should not be hidden away; they are a great learning opportunity for everyone in the company, so unless you are working on something very confidential you should keep as many people as possible aware of any progress.

**5** Be clear on the time frame for pilot projects. People invest a lot of time, energy and emotion in nurturing ideas, so it is important that everyone understands pilots that do not reach certain milestones will be terminated. You have a finite capacity to test new ideas, so you must make tough decisions, particularly if continuing a pilot is preventing another more lucrative idea being pursued. People can become emotionally attached to ideas, so there is a risk that time and energy is spread too thinly across a multitude of mini pilots that never fully mature.

For creativity and innovation to prosper, it helps if there is a process to follow, otherwise the ideas never become anything more concrete than wishful thinking. A really innovative team will turn good ideas into an action plan swiftly.

The steps in the process are outlined below.

# Prepare the groundwork for innovation

One way to create space and time for innovation is to set up dedicated sessions for brainstorming or creative problem solving. To set up your session for success, it is imperative to lay the foundation and ground rules for the day. Enable those attending the session to be successful, by providing them with as much information as possible in advance on the format and objective of the session.

It is a good idea to appoint a facilitator. An external facilitator is often the best option, as it enables you and the team members to focus on the activity, rather than the coordination of the day.

Once you have the session arranged, clearly define the challenge that you are trying to solve. Ensure that everyone understands the problem, and what success looks like in terms of an outcome.

In advance of the session, and during if appropriate, it is important that everyone has access to all the relevant data and information. If there is sensitive data or new information that you can't circulate beforehand, then take time at the beginning of the meeting to brief everyone.

Explain the process to the team and agree the desired behaviours in advance. It is important that everyone understands what is expected of them in terms of behaviours and contributions, both in the meeting and at each subsequent stage of the process. Some people will be very good at seeing the pitfalls of an idea, which is a very useful skill; but the real value comes from those who can see the pitfalls *and* provide solutions. Focusing too early in the process on why an idea might not work can kill creativity and get in the way of finding an innovative solution.

## Create options

Suspend judgement and allow the team time to brainstorm options and ideas. At this stage, the team should aim to build upon an option or idea, and criticisms should be parked. It is OK for team members to question an option for the purposes of increasing their understanding, but not to scrutinize it.

To facilitate the inclusion of both introverts and extroverts, it is good to start the option generation process as individuals; for example, you could get people to write their ideas on Post-It notes. This will ensure that the introverts get the opportunity to get their ideas across before the extroverts fill the air with their ideas. Have everyone put their ideas up on a whiteboard or stick Post-Its to the wall, then categorize the ideas into common themes. Take time to ensure that everyone understands each idea.

## Reflect on the options

Having generated the options, now is the time to look and see whether there are common themes between ideas – or if different ideas could be merged to form a 'super idea'. It is important at this point to nurture ideas, so ensure the group focuses on the question 'What would it take to make this idea a success?' Remaining positive is critical. The time will come later to identify risks.

Here is one easy method of evaluation: score each idea from 1–5 on two separate factors:

**A**  Ease of implementation (1 = hard to implement; 5 = easy to implement).

**B**  Scale of benefit/impact (1 = low benefit/impact; 5 = high benefit/impact).

The total score for each idea is derived by multiplying A × B.

In this system, an idea with a score of 20–25 will be relatively easy to implement and deliver a major benefit, meaning these ideas should be prioritized for action first. Those that attract a score of 15–20 also deserve attention, but may be scheduled only after the other high-scoring initiatives have been completed.

## Identify the risks

As mentioned above, identifying risks is an extremely important part of any business leader's job. However, the really successful business people not only identify the risks but also put forward ideas to mitigate the risks.

It is at this stage of the process that the team members get to be critical or express reservations about ideas. The team needs to realize that being risk averse or being a risk taker is not inherently good or bad; it is simply a reflection of one's appetite for risk. It is usually good to remind the group of possible feelings or tensions that may arise at this point; sometimes people can feel defensive of their ideas in the face of criticism, or others may feel bad about raising objections or doubts. You can help mitigate this by reminding your team that risk assessment such as this is an incredibly valuable part of the process, to make the ideas the best ideas they can possibly be.

You may find it helpful to remind people that the purpose of identifying risks is not to shoot down any ideas, but to commence the process of mitigating any risks. Really successful business people can see and swiftly mitigate risks, and thus take action before their competition. Remember, if you choose not to take an action because the risks are perceived to be too high, then you may leave the option open for your competition to seize the opportunity.

## *Prioritize the options*

Having identified the benefit potential and associated risk, it is now time to prioritize and select the ideas to be taken forward for piloting or implementation. At this point it is useful to look back at the success criteria you outlined for the day and what the 'to be' outcome looks like for each of the challenges addressed in the session. Those ideas that look best positioned to deliver the greatest benefit, in the shortest period of time, with the lowest risk, should be prioritized for immediate action.

## *Develop an action plan*

Now is the time to decide whether to develop a pilot or small-scale trial, or whether to implement the idea straight away. Whatever option is chosen will probably require an implementation project of some description with an appropriately skilled project manager.

The key aspects of developing an action plan will revolve around the following:

**1** Setting a vision for what success from the initiative looks like.

**2** An understanding of how success will be measured.

**3** Assigning adequate resources with the right skills and competencies.

**4** Ensuring those resources have the time to devote to delivering a successful outcome.

**5** A timeline for key deliverables and milestones.

The final step is to secure senior management support, and agree how progress will be communicated to both senior management and the wider organization.

---

### Tips, tricks and takeaways

- **Innovation models:** in order to make the most of the innovation process, it may be worthwhile using tried and tested innovation models such as the de Bono Hats (de Bono, 1985) or mind mapping (Buzan, 1993).

### Reflective exercise

Think about the last business problem that came up in your work, or that of your team or company. This could be anything from a new product from a competitor or one of your vendors raising their prices, to a colleague being unexpectedly off sick, to needing to think of ways to develop new business.

What was the process for solving it? Did you just take the first available solution? Ignore the problem completely in favour of your day-to-day work? Was an innovation process implemented? How well did it work?

Using the recommendations in the chapter, jot down some ideas for how the problem-solving process could have been made more innovative.

# References

Buzan, T (1993) *The Mind Map Book*, Penguin, New York
de Bono, E (1985) *Six Thinking Hats*, Little, Brown and Company, New York

## 22
# Bringing about behavioural change

Initiating behavioural change in an individual, team or organization is not easy, especially if you want the change to be sustained. Achieving lasting behavioural change rarely happens quickly and is usually a gradual progression – like developing a new habit. Before any change can take place, the individual or team needs to recognize why the change is required, see the value in changing and be prepared to prioritize making the change happen. In other words, although there are things you can do to drive and motivate behavioural change, ultimately it has to come from them.

## Our process for change

The process outlined below has six steps, which focus on the preparation for change, the actual change occurring and the post-change period, to ensure that the change endures and becomes the new norm:

1 Understand the need for change.

2 Envision the desired end state.

3 Prepare for implementation: focus and plan.

4 Implementation: take action.

5 Relapse prevention: don't be tempted to abandon the change.

6 Embed the change: measure, recognize and reward.

### Understand the need for change

Being ready to change is important. Change is rarely successful when sprung on people – this may be a catalyst for action to happen, but lasting change is brought about as a result of considered decision making and ensuring the time is right.

Change is an action-oriented activity. It is never passive; everyone involved must be prepared to take action, otherwise no real change will take place. Realizing this is important – for example, many people know they should exercise more and eat more healthily, but not everyone actually takes the action to do something about it. This means that securing a commitment to act is critical.

Ask these questions to those participating in the process:

- How will *you* know when you have achieved the change?
- How will *others* know you have successfully changed?
- What are the consequences of not changing the behaviour?

Always talk about the change in the terms of the impact. For example, a football coach taking players through punishing fitness programmes will continually reinforce that fitter players have a greater chance of winning: they will focus on the outcome of being fitter, rather than simply being fit for the sake of it. The coach will also point out the likely outcome of not maintaining and improving fitness: in this example, skipping the training programmes would lead to the increased likelihood of losing the game due to getting tired.

Likewise, in a business context, it is important that the team understand the outcomes of the change – both the benefits of taking action and the risks associated with not taking action. Like the coach in the example, you can point out the consequences or risks inherent in persevering with the status quo, and paint a picture of a 'better place' where the participants will either feel more secure or receive some material benefit as a result of the change.

## *Envision the desired end state*

Taking the focus on outcomes one step further, in order to drive behavioural change, a leader needs to be clear on the desired end state. Everyone involved should be able to illustrate succinctly the difference between the current situation and what that they are trying to create. Strong leaders always bring clarity to a change scenario; being able to clearly communicate the desired end state in a manner that will resonate with the audience is critical. A good test for this might be explaining the change, the need for change and the desired outcome or end state – in plain words – to an unconnected third party. Imagine you have to communicate your rationale to the 'ordinary person on the street'; if this seems impossible, or your third party is failing to grasp your point, then you may need to consider refining your vision. Consider illustrating your explanation with an example business scenario.

Taking time to ensure that everyone involved is aware of the desired end state will be invaluable in getting their commitment to making the change happen. This is a huge factor in the likelihood of the change being successful; when the leader and key influencers in the group are publicly committed to the change, the more junior group members will be more likely to follow as they see this commitment at the top.

## Focus and plan

Having decided to commence the process of behavioural change, and become clear on the desired end state, it is important to approach the change in a focused manner. Take the time to map out the journey and timeline from the current situation to where you want to be. This phase is important, because everyone involved in the change must be able to see the rate of expected progression and know there is a plan in place.

Avoid the temptation to do everything at once, as an overambitious behavioural change strategy is highly unlikely to work – people become overwhelmed and cannot sustain the changes made. Instead, plan to make the overall change in a series of manageable chunks, starting with a few quick wins to create momentum. If you attempt the most difficult aspect of the change at the outset, you or the team may again find it overwhelming. If you instead build up some positive energy and goodwill by tackling some easier tasks first, you may find the team will have gained confidence from the early wins and will feel less daunted.

## Take action

In essence, behavioural change is the process of trying to break a habit and create a new habit at the same time. Depending on who you listen to, creating a habit requires a significant amount of repetition – the theories vary, but one such example is that consistent action is required every day for at least 20 consecutive days.

The key thing to remember when relating this to behavioural change is that it is all about actions – you cannot make a theoretical behavioural change; you must act out the change and visibly demonstrate to yourself and others that the new behaviour is going to flourish. Many people talk a good game when it comes to change, but few are actually successful in bringing about the change because they focus on the theory rather than the actions. This is why your plan is so important.

Determine your actions within these guidelines:

- What concrete actions will you take in the next seven days to bring about your behavioural change?
- What will be the impact of the change?
- How are you measuring the change?
- When do you expect to see the impact of the change?
- When will others see the impact or benefit of the change?

## Don't be tempted to abandon the change

Behavioural change is not easy, and it is likely that an opportunity to relapse into old ways will present itself along the way. It is a good idea to take the time to identify in advance the triggers that may bring about a relapse – it could be a particular situation, an event, or even an individual who could tempt you or your team to revert to old habits.

It helps enormously if you have planned in advance how you will respond if the opportunity to regress presents itself. If you have anticipated the risk of relapse and recognize the triggers, then you will be well prepared to respond positively and stay true to your long-term goal.

## Measure, recognize and reward

Behavioural change will be sustained only if the progress is measured, recognized and rewarded – this is true even for individual changes, where you must recognize and reward yourself. The importance of recognition cannot be overstated; take every opportunity to recognize the individual(s) or team when you see measurable progress towards the goal. As behavioural change is hard, people need to be encouraged and the simple act of recognizing progress can do wonders for motivation to continue the process.

## Tips, tricks and takeaways

- **Resistance:** if you find that the team is not embracing change, it may be due to a lack of motivation. You either have to make the future state more attractive, or make the consequences of not changing starker and the current state less attractive.

- **Stay strong in the tough times:** it is easy to model behavioural change when times are good, which is why most members of the group won't truly believe that the leader has changed until they see them react under pressure.

- **Make your goal consistent:** the change you are trying to bring about must also be aligned with the company strategy and culture. If there is inconsistency between the desired behavioural change and the company culture, then it is unlikely the change will be sustained over time.

## Reflective exercise

Think about a change you would like to see. Ideally this would be a workplace or business example, but you could also think of a change you would like to see in your own life – fitness or health habits, for example.

Now think about how you could bring about this change in a practical way that will last:

- What are the tangible benefits of the change (both hard and soft benefits)?

- Who will benefit from the change, and how?

- What are the critical success criteria of the change – what are the key points that must be true for you to know the change has been a success?

- When does the impact of the change need to be noticeable to stakeholders?

- What might be the factors that will enable this change?

- What might be the barriers to this change?

- Who are your allies (ie people who will support you on this journey)?

- Who might not support the change? Why – what might their objections be?

- How might you persuade the detractors to become supporters? Try to think of specific actions.

# 23
# Overcoming resistance

Resistance will not always manifest itself in an obvious way. Most people are positively disposed towards being agreeable, so the resistance may be hidden by a pleasant manner. Resistance can also be disguised as agreement: people might say something like 'That's a great idea, and we should also do X, Y and Z'. Although this sounds positive on the surface, all it actually does is increase the scope of the change or project, thus turning the idea into an impossible initiative that will never get off the ground.

## Where is this resistance coming from?

It is always good to flush out any underlying anxiety within a group. The root cause of most resistance can usually be attributed to one or a combination of the following:

### Lack of clarity

People will almost always display resistance if they do not have a clear picture of the goals or benefits that will accrue from the activity, so it is important that everyone understands what success looks like before you start the initiative. In this respect, everyone must understand the current situation – sometimes for people to be motivated to address change or achieve the goal, you must outline the existing position and the benefits of a positive future state.

### Fear of the unknown

If you are being very innovative or the path to achieving your objectives is unclear, you will probably encounter resistance. If something is very new, there can be a natural reticence or nervousness. Fear of the unknown is reasonable – it shows that people care and are thinking about the consequences or collateral damage.

Your skill as a leader will be to make people feel comfortable with the risk in adopting the new process. The best thing to do is acknowledge the reality, empathize and help people to overcome their concerns. In acknowledging the reality, you make people feel heard – and you can elicit from that what they require to build their confidence.

Fear of the unknown usually manifests itself in either overly fastidious attention to detail (which hinders progress) or endless talking about the topic rather than taking action. It is important when dealing with a fear to make people feel confident in their own ability and the collective strength of the team.

## Fear of failure

Sometimes people will fully understand you and what you want to achieve but will be apprehensive about being associated with something that might fail. Essentially, they are risk averse. Being risk averse is not an inherently good or bad attribute; ultimately, as the leader you have to help people take ownership of actions to help mitigate their fears. To help overcome a fear of failure, be sure to create time and space to adequately address risks and issues that may be influencing the team or individual's confidence.

## A desire to preserve the status quo

The status quo exists for a reason; it may be a comfort zone, or it may be that people still value the benefits associated with the current way of doing things, which makes them reluctant to proceed. Often in established organizations, people will have a vested interest in maintaining the status quo because they were probably instrumental in building it. Their affinity with the way things are may be because they see it as their legacy or a manifestation of their hard work. As a result, sometimes it is good to bring the past with you – find a way to recognize the status quo for what it meant to the company's current success. Avoid the desire to be dismissive or critical, but try to think about it as something that was appropriate at a particular point in time. You may well be able to do this by showing how the benefits of the status quo will be preserved or enhanced in the future.

## An inability to see 'what's in it for me?'

People will not be motivated to leave their comfort zone unless they can clearly see 'what's in it for me?' You need to present your vision in a manner that makes it clear to those in your audience what the benefits will be for them.

Many leaders spend time focusing on the benefits to the company, without being explicit about how those benefits will filter down to individuals or teams. It is important to personalize the message and make the positive impact clear at an individual level – your message must be compelling to the individual.

## Conflicting priorities

Individuals will exhibit resistance if they are currently working towards and being rewarded for an alternative priority or goal, especially if your project or initiative could undermine their other priority. It is not unusual for teams within companies to have mutually exclusive goals. This is done to drive innovation and a balanced outcome: for example, the sales teams are incentivized to sell more units, while operations are incentivized to save money by reducing stock or minimizing distribution costs. These separate goals encourage the individuals to behave differently, and that difference in approach may manifest itself as resistance.

# How can I reduce resistance?

The best way to reduce resistance is to involve key people in the design and implementation of the 'to be' model. You want those people who are most likely to present resistance to feel ownership for the success of the initiative. It is good to identify who the key influencers are in the organization, and involve them early in the project.

The worst type of resistance is the resistance you can't see, so it is also good to facilitate forums where resistance or objections can be brought to the surface. One good approach is to set up sessions with groups of employees offering them the opportunity to express their hopes and fears. It is important that you respond in a supportive manner to those who express fears. A good way to solicit any underlying fears is to ask people to write them on Post-It notes and then stick the notes up on a wall or whiteboard, so that they can be categorized into themes and no one person feels singled out.

The next action is to put in place a plan to address the concerns that have been raised. Be positive and encouraging, because now that you can see the resistance, you have a better chance of addressing it successfully. If you react negatively, you will push the resistance underground, thus making it almost impossible to deal with.

If you have done your best to eliminate the resistance and it is not subsiding, then you may have to make a tough choice – either you stop the initiative, or you take steps to remove the resisters.

An important question to ask is: are you the source of the resistance? Sometimes the leader can create the resistance by displaying the following behaviours:

- being overly critical;

- forcing an overly rigid structure;

- putting yourself forward as being all-knowing and being unwilling to accept input, questions or criticism;

- failure to create an environment conducive to change.

The above factors may be particularly true if you – at the same time as demonstrating these behaviours – require your team to be innovative in finding a long-term solution.

## Tips, tricks and takeaways

- **Use the grapevine:** tap into informal information networks to assess how people are feeling about work in general, and your initiative in particular. If your access to the grapevine is limited, you could solicit support from someone else.

- **Build trust:** think about setting up a casual social evening with the team, so that you can get to know them on a personal level and build trust and confidence in an informal setting.

- **Risk assessment:** set up a formal risk evaluation exercise where people are encouraged to bring forward any and all misgivings or fears they hold about the initiative. You might also get them to suggest what would make them feel more comfortable with the change.

- **Use key influencers:** identify key influencers and get them to talk to those who may be showing resistance.

- **Engage senior management support:** if necessary, can you get senior management to mandate that the initiative is important, and make it clear they have an expectation that the team will collaborate to make the project a success?

- **Share the big picture:** everyone needs to understand the bigger picture. Individuals will be reluctant to embrace change if they don't understand or appreciate the context in which they are operating. No matter how junior or removed from the customer an individual is, it is important that they understand how they contribute to the overall customer experience and, therefore, the success of the company. People are much more likely to embrace change if they see it as part of a much bigger endeavour.

## Reflective exercise

It may be worth assessing the balance between the forces of resistance and the desire to drive the change. Think about an idea you have that has met with resistance in the past:

- Who were the forces behind the resistance?
- Who were the supportive forces?
- Which group force outweighed the other?

Now that you have identified those who were resistant, rank them from most influential to least influential.

What could you have done to help address their resistance? How did you deal with it at the time? What might you do differently now?

# PART THREE
# Managing the task

# 24
# How to interview (as a candidate)

*This chapter assumes you are an **external candidate**; however, most of the points are relevant even if you are an internal candidate. The main difference to be aware of if you're an internal candidate is that there is a better chance that the interviewers will already know you and your work.*

Interviewing is your opportunity to get face-to-face with a key decision-maker in the company and bring your CV to life with more detail and explanation.

While not every interviewee lands the job, the interview experience itself is excellent for building your confidence, honing your pitch and discovering what exactly employers are looking for in the current market – which is particularly useful if you are making a move after a long period of time with one employer.

## Before the interview

**Research the role:** try to make contact with people you know who either do a similar role for the hiring company or a similar role in another company. Ask them to share their view of the culture within the company and the expectations of the role. Specifically, you want to discover what the hiring company is looking for. Don't assume they are always looking for the best and brightest; sometimes if a role is repetitive or unlikely to allow for change they will look for a person who likes stability and consistency and is likely to stay in the role. A 'high flyer' may become bored within six months and leave.

**Research the company:** What is the recent history of the company? How is it performing in the industry? What is the CEO or management team focused on for the immediate future? Are there any risks, such as rumoured takeovers or lawsuits, that would damage the company? If possible, ask a customer for their view of the company. What are the company values and how does it demonstrate that it lives by its values? Increasingly companies are checking whether or not the candidate will fit with the company's values and culture. For many people it is the company's values that provide the unique sense of purpose that will inspire them to stay and grow with a company. Make sure your values are aligned with the company values.

> Tip: if you are an internal candidate, research the team or area that has the vacancy.

**Research the industry:** What is going on in the industry? Who are the big players? What are the risks and opportunities for the industry as a whole? Will the company you are interviewing with be a winner or loser over time? This point is particularly relevant with the rapid pace of change in technology; some industries may become irrelevant in the future.

If you are an internal candidate you will be expected to show an understanding of the environment within which the team and company operate – show you have taken the time to solicit an 'outside in' perspective.

> Tip: assess the dress code. If in doubt, it's better to overdress for the interview than be too casual.

# In the interview

The golden rule in the interview is to be yourself! When you are being yourself you are much more likely to be relaxed and to come across as a genuine individual. If you try to be someone that you are not, or pretend to be something that you are not, you run the risk of coming across as inauthentic.

Remember, even if you are offered the role you will have to go through a probation period, during which time your true self will emerge. You won't be able to keep up a pretence for this period of time without putting yourself under immense stress.

It is never wise to lie or stretch the truth in an interview, as inevitably it will come back to haunt you and may even compromise your integrity. Be true to yourself.

In an interview process the interviewer is trying to identify the candidate that will be most suitable for the role. To do this, the interview will fundamentally break down to three key questions:

- **Can you do the role?** Do you have the capability, skills, competencies and experience to do the role?

- **Will you do the role?** Will you bring drive, passion and energy to the role that will inspire others to do their best work?

- **Will you fit in?** Is your style compatible with the culture of the team or organization? Will you enhance the morale or 'vibe' within the team?

## Answer the question you are asked

Some candidates are desperate to show all that they know and give long, detailed answers. Instead, give a clear and concise answer to the question. When you are finished, ask the interviewer if they would like more detail, rather than assuming they want a very detailed answer upfront. Sense-check the depth of detail with the interviewer – you don't want the interviewer to conclude that you ramble or are unstructured in your communication style.

If you don't know the answer to a question, acknowledge the reality and explain why you cannot answer the question. Do not be tempted to wing it as that may undermine your credibility in all other questions.

Your answer should contain four parts:

**1** Provide some context (be brief).

**2** Elaborate on what actions *you* took: illustrate the process you went through and what competencies you exhibited to deliver the results.

**3** Summarize the result or impact you had in the context of benefits in the following areas:

    **a** revenue generation or cost reduction;

    **b** improvement in customer experience;

    **c** risk mitigation or compliance improvement;

    **d** process improvement;

    **e** development of others.

**4** Explain why the example you chose is relevant to the job you are applying for, ie the example should give you the opportunity to illustrate how you demonstrated the behaviours and competencies that are highlighted in the job description.

## Be enthusiastic

You want to come across as passionate and committed, but not desperate for the role. Interviewers will be looking for someone to bring life to the role and to their team, so share the reason for your enthusiasm in the interview.

## Positive attitude

It is very important to display a positive attitude. Avoid the temptation of being overly critical of the past or the status quo; focus your answers on the positive aspects of your response to the question. Do not be tempted to talk down or criticize your current employer, your competitors or other individuals.

To illustrate the point here are two answers to a standard interview question: Why do you want to leave your current employer/role?

**1** **Sample positive answer:** 'I am keen to develop myself and grow professionally. My research indicates that your company has a great culture, is doing well and offers the best route for me to fulfil my career aspirations. My current employer has been good to me, but is not as well positioned right now to offer the type of long-term career opportunities that you can.'

**2** **Sample negative answer:** 'The company isn't doing very well, there are very few opportunities and there is a general feeling of uncertainty that is having a negative impact on morale – so it is time for me to move on.'

The second answer is not good for the following reasons:

- It criticizes your current employer in public, showing you to be indiscreet.
- It implies that you are more motivated to leave your current employer than excited to join the new company.
- It gives the impression that you see yourself as a victim or are walking away from a challenge.

## Ensure you understand the question

If you don't understand a question it is reasonable to ask for some context or for the interviewer to elaborate so that you can give a considered answer.

## Conflict

Be prepared to answer a question about how you deal with conflict. Specifically, be ready to talk through a scenario about a time where you had a fundamental disagreement with another individual. Talk about what actions you took to try to resolve the conflict. How did you engage constructively to understand the other person's point of view and how did you share your perspective? Did you involve other people? If so when and how did you involve other people? What was the end result? It is OK if the scenario ended up with you both agreeing to disagree, but you need to show that the disagreement was managed professionally and did not adversely impact the business or others on the team. Ideally, you will be able to illustrate that the counter arguments were put forward in a businesslike manner and not as personal attacks on the other person's opinion or point of view.

## Dealing with disappointment

Be prepared to answer a question on how you reacted to a situation that did not turn out as you had hoped. The key thing is to illustrate what you learnt from the experience and how you have applied that learning in subsequent situations. Be sure not to cast yourself as a victim in the scenario; retain ownership for the outcome, as this illustrates your leadership calibre and willingness to take responsibility.

## Your developmental needs

Showing a thirst for continual learning and development is extremely important. High-performing leaders and members of high-performing teams will always take time out to reflect and consider what could have been done differently to achieve a better result. Having an open mind to learning opportunities is a key competency. Having the self-awareness to understand what areas you want to develop is also important. Be prepared to answer a question on your development needs, articulate clearly why you have prioritized the areas you have chosen. Remember it is OK to choose to strengthen a strength as opposed to address a weakness.

## *Have a few questions prepared*

In most interviews you will be invited to ask a question at some stage, so it is good to have a few questions prepared. The questions should be non-confrontational and relatively easy for the interviewer to answer, such as a question that focuses on the company culture, opportunities for career growth and professional development, or how success will be measured in the role.

Be careful not to ask a question that you should know the answer to – don't ask a question that could easily be answered by looking at the company website or looking at the annual report, for example, as this may show you did not bother to research the company.

Your question should be relevant and genuine; don't use it as an opportunity to make a point or show off. You can build on your research by asking questions that occurred to you during your preparation, and referencing your research in those questions. Don't ask a very technical question unless the interviewer has the appropriate skills. Don't ask about confidential topics or a question that could be construed negatively, such as the recent loss of a customer or any bad news topics you came across in the media. You can save those questions until after you have been offered the job.

## *Missing competency*

If you feel that you have a competency or skill set that was not discussed during the interview, it is OK to point this out to the interviewer. One way to do this might be when you are offered the chance to ask a question. You could say 'Before I ask a question may I just take this opportunity, as it didn't come up in our discussion, to mention that I do have competency X or experience Y, which I believe from the job description is important'.

# After the interview

If you feel there are topics that were not discussed at the interview that may help your case in the selection process, it can be appropriate to send a follow-up email to the interviewer and/or HR recruiter providing the additional information. Be careful that the follow up is not considered as 'canvassing'.

Don't be afraid to ask for feedback. If you do not get offered the role or invited to the next round of interviews, it is important to ask for feedback. When you get the response, thank the individual for the experience and digest the feedback – but never challenge it.

# How to handle a group interview

Some companies ask candidates to participate in group interviews. Candidates will usually be given a brief (some candidates may be given slightly different briefs) and asked to find a solution to a problem or make a recommendation. There is usually no right answer to the problem presented; however, the company will ask the group to make a recommendation. The company won't be focusing on what answer you come up with, but more on how you came to your conclusion.

Inevitably the company will be looking for candidates who display the ability to:

- present a compelling point of view;
- build up on the ideas of others;
- be inclusive – draw introverts into the conversation;
- demonstrate active listening, show empathy to other perspectives;
- compromise or look constructively for an accommodation with someone who has an alternative perspective;
- keep the conversation on track, both in terms of time and adherence to topic;
- summarize the key points or decisions made at the end of the meeting.

Be careful not to dominate the conversation. Don't get hung up on the answer to the question; focus more on the behaviours you display both verbally and non-verbally. For example, if the group doesn't adopt your idea or suggestion, don't sulk or withdraw from the discussion.

## *Competency-based interviews*

In a competency-based interview, candidates will be asked to give an example of how they had to use a specific competency. You'll be expected to give an overview of the scenario, how you displayed the competency and what outcome was achieved. It is always good to be able to illustrate what you learnt from the experience. An example of competency-based questions are as follows:

- **Action oriented:** Tell me about an initiative you worked on that had an extremely tight timeline. How did you proceed? What did you do to ensure a successful outcome?

- **Composure:** Tell me about a time when you were extremely frustrated. How did you work through the situation?

- **Integrity:** Tell me about a time when you had to make a decision that required you to be scrupulously fair. What did you do? What was the outcome?

- **Problem solving:** Tell me about the most challenging problem you have had to solve in work. What was your approach? What was the outcome?

- **Planning:** Tell me about a major project or initiative you had to lead or were involved in. What was your role? What approach did you take? What would you do differently if you had the opportunity to turn back time?

- **Customer focus:** How do you handle unhappy customers? What approach do you take to find out whether your customers are happy?

## Tips, tricks and takeaways

- **Dress code:** assess the dress code that is most likely in place at the company you are interviewing with. If in doubt, overdress for the interview.

- **Experience interviews:** in an interview that is focusing on experience, candidates will be asked to give an in-depth account of their experience and illustrate how that experience will be relevant for the advertised role. The candidate will be expected to be able to illustrate how they applied their experience in a number of different scenarios. For example, how have you been able to transfer the benefit of your experience to those who work with you? What impact did this have?

- **Apparently 'odd' questions:** it is not unusual for interviewers to ask non-standard questions such as the following:

o Which film star/famous person would you most like to have dinner with?

o Which world leader do you respect the most?

o If you won the lottery tomorrow, what would you do?

- Don't feel under pressure to give a quick off-the-cuff answer; it is perfectly OK to say that you haven't thought about the question and then ask for time to consider your answer. Keep your answer reasonably conservative – the interviewer is probably more interested in your approach to answering the question rather than the answer itself.

## Reflective exercise

- Give some thought to identifying your values and how you would like to live by your values.

- How will this role or company help as you strive to live by your values?

- Can you articulate your values in a clear, concise manner?

- Can you provide examples of how you made decisions based upon your values?

- Try to arrange with a mentor or coach to do a mock interview. A mock interview is a fabulous way to practise your answers, which also enables you to hear yourself answer questions.

# 25
# Performance discussions (as an employee)

A well-structured performance discussion can be a wonderful development experience that will enable you to think strategically about your career. Not all companies run a disciplined performance management process, so if you are lucky enough to work for a company that does, be sure to make the most of the opportunity. A good performance discussion will give you a perspective on how you operate, and suggest areas where you could do things differently to have a greater impact in your current role or accelerate career progression. In some cases, this may mean further developing a competency that is already a strength, or it may mean acquiring more experience or improving a perceived deficiency. No matter what the outcome, it is important to remember that you own and control your development – so enter the exercise with an open mind.

## When you are performing well

Prepare for the meeting and be very clear what you want to achieve both in the short term and the long term. Reasonable questions for you to consider in advance of the meeting include the following:

- What do I want in the long term?
- What is the ideal next role for me? What will it give me to enhance my chances of further career progression?
- What do you see as your development needs? Decide whether you want to address a weakness or improve a strength, and assess which will have the bigger impact on your long-term career. Many people focus on

addressing a weakness, but sometimes it is better to invest time in improving a strength.

- Have you thought about what kind of support you want? Is it educational assistance, both in terms of financial support and time off to study? Do you want more responsibility? Do you want support in attending industry conferences and seminars? More time off to participate on boards or on industry bodies? Job rotation? Greater exposure to senior management?

- Are you prepared to travel?

In preparation for the meeting, make an inventory of all the great things you have delivered over the last 12 months and link them to the impact on the company. You want to help your boss to help you, and reminding them of how productive you are is helpful.

Be prepared to give your boss a cogent and succinct overview of where you see yourself going and what you want from them. The more specific you can be, the easier it is for your boss to help.

In the performance discussion, some questions for your boss include:

- What does the company see as my career path? In small companies this may involve a route to equity ownership.

- What is the company going to do to support my continued professional development?

- Where is the company going?

- Is your boss thinking of moving on and, if so, would you be likely to get his/her role? If the answer is that you would not get their role, then get very specific feedback about what you would have to do to be considered for the role (assuming you want it). As this could potentially be a sensitive or personal question, it must be broached sensitively; but it should not be avoided. You need to understand if your progression is being blocked through no fault of your own and you and the company need to have a mature conversation about other opportunities for progression.

# When you are not performing well

If you feel that you are not performing to the required standard, it is important to be honest with yourself. A career is a marathon, not a sprint; most people will hit a bump in the road at some stage. It is important to reflect and try to learn from the experience, and also to assess whether the situation is recoverable.

Are you in the right frame of mind to receive feedback? If you feel that now is not a good time, it may be possible to reschedule the meeting.

Are you sure of what you want to achieve or learn from the performance review meeting?

A performance review meeting is a two-way street, so be sure to provide feedback if you feel that you are not getting the support you need to be successful. Have examples to illustrate the point.

The questions below may help to orient your thoughts:

- What is going on for me in my life and in my role?
- Am I truly happy in the role?
- If there were no constraints, what would I do next?
- Am I in a job that makes the most of what I have to give?
- Do I want to do what it takes to turn the situation around?
- Should I pursue an alternative career strategy?

In the performance discussion, remember:

- **Be positive:** the person giving you the feedback is ultimately trying to help you, even though it may not feel like it at the time. By giving you difficult feedback, your manager is actually giving you what you need and showing that they are invested in supporting you. The easy thing for them to do is say nothing, but by choosing to give you the feedback they are showing that they care about you.

- **Listen with an open mind:** listen to understand the feedback; do not become defensive in the meeting. If you feel the feedback is unreasonable, simply state that you feel it is unreasonable and say that you will provide a written response after the meeting.

- **Explore alternatives:** What would happen if you had different responsibilities or if inhibitors to your high performance were removed?

Following the meeting, there are some key points to tackle that can help solidify your position:

- **Seek out a third party:** discuss the feedback, as well as your feelings on getting that feedback.

- **Own the feedback:** avoid the temptation to blame the person giving you the feedback or conclude that they are somehow wrong – often, the feedback they give is their opinion, so it cannot be right or wrong. You don't have to agree with the feedback but it is helpful to understand it. Remember, it is unlikely the person giving the feedback is the only person who has that view of you, but even if they are, it is helpful to know that this is how you are perceived by your manager. Let them know that you will own the feedback, and that you would like their support in addressing it going forward.

- **Sum it up:** ask for a written summary of the meeting, including what is expected of you and a timeline within which you can try to turn the situation around.

- **Prioritize your next steps:** Is there anything you can do immediately that would have a swift positive impact? Identify three things you are going to do differently as a result of the feedback, then share those three things with the person who gave you the feedback to make sure that your proposed actions are what the person was hoping for.

- **Follow up:** request a follow-up meeting for 4–6 weeks' time to discuss your progress.

- **Is it time to make a move?** If need be, look to see if you can part ways amicably with the company. Some companies will enter into a separation agreement that will include an extended period (ie longer than statutory notice) for the individual to seek employment elsewhere.

Whatever you decide, do not burn bridges. If you gossip or behave in an unreasonable manner, you run the risk of undermining your future success. For further reading, see Chapter 9 on dealing with disappointing news.

---

## Tips, tricks and takeaways

- **Be future focused:** while it is important to reflect upon the past to garner learning, the real value in the discussion is in determining the best course of action to take for the future.

- **Keep emotional distance:** try not to take the feedback personally. We all have opportunities to improve, so take the feedback for what it is, and then make a calm and rational decision on what you are going to do about it. Remember: you always own the response to feedback.

- **Don't make assumptions:** if you don't fully understand the feedback, go back to your boss and ask for more detail.

### Reflective exercise

Write down your top three achievements and top three learning points from the last 12 months or review period.

What might you do to build upon your achievements? What could you do differently as a result of the learning?

Practise discussing your approach with a colleague or friend. Ask the person to pay attention to your language and tone.

# 26
# One-to-one meetings with your boss

Regular, well-structured, one-to-one meetings are beneficial in a professional environment, as they enable clear communication and a collaborative working relationship between you and your boss or you and your direct reports.

But the one-to-one meeting can be a challenge. The focus of the one-to-one meeting with your boss will vary over time, meaning you might find it daunting or not fully utilize the allotted time.

## Planning is key

The key to a good one-to-one discussion is preparation.

Sometimes you want your boss's opinion or direction; sometimes you want to simply brief or update them on what is important for you and your team. Alternatively, you may want to brainstorm longer-term strategic topics. Sometimes the meeting will be devoted to an in-depth discussion of one topic; on other occasions you may cover multiple topics. The important thing is to plan and be specific on the outcome you want to achieve from the time available – whatever the overarching purpose of the meeting. The planning may indicate that you will need to set up another meeting to discuss a specific topic or issue.

The questions below help in preparing a one-to-one agenda. I would suggest altering the order depending upon what is most critical for you at the appropriate time; I am not suggesting that you cover all of the topics below in one meeting, but as a rule of thumb, you should aim to cover each topic at least once every few months:

- **Top of mind:** What needs to be discussed now or as a matter of urgency?

- **Help wanted:** be specific on what you need from your boss to enable you to remove a block or assist you in achieving a goal.

- **Latent issues:** list areas that you do not need specific assistance with or need to discuss but that you feel your boss should be aware of.

- **Achievements:** What have you or your team delivered since the last meeting? This question acts as a method of evaluating your impact – if you cannot list deliverables that you or your team are proud of, at least quarterly, it suggests that perhaps you are being ineffective or are not contributing to meaningful outcomes/deliverables.

- **Key short-term focus:** (ie this quarter) list the key actions you and your team are focusing on right now.

- **Risks:** What are you not focusing on? Where are you falling behind? What commitments are at risk of not being delivered? When raising a risk, always include what you are doing to mitigate the risk, or details of what specific help you need to mitigate the risk.

- **People:** How is the team developing? Who is performing well? Do you have concerns about any individuals? Any recognition you want your boss to give to a team member? Any key anniversaries or life events impacting team members?

- **Performance feedback:** always check in regularly on performance – is there anything your boss would like you to do differently or do more of?

- **Your own development:** as part of checking in on your own performance it is also important to seek feedback on what skills, competencies and experience your boss feels you should develop to progress in your career. Solicit practical support from your boss for your development goals. For example, sponsorship on courses, involvement in projects or assignments that will give you the right level of experience and exposure to be your best self.

## Tips, tricks and takeaways

- **Be specific:** in advance of the meeting always be specific on what you want to achieve. Ask yourself: what constitutes a successful outcome?

- **Be prepared:** send your proposed agenda to your boss well in advance of the meeting. In as much as the value of the meeting is significantly determined by your preparation, it is also influenced by your manager's preparation – so the more time they have to prepare the better.

- **Soliciting your boss's support:** there is a real skill in being able to anticipate issues and take preventative actions; you need to solicit help and support at a point that gives your boss enough time to have the desired impact, and not leave it until the last possible minute. A regular one-to-one meeting is a good place to raise early concerns in this way.

- **Frequency:** this will vary according to the nature of the role, but it is probably good to have a one-to-one at least every two weeks. The one-to-one should be scheduled as a recurring meeting and both parties should make a commitment to attend. In the event of one party being unavailable, the meeting should be rescheduled as opposed to cancelled.

- **Duration:** it is probably good to schedule an hour for a one-to-one meeting. If you don't cover everything, then schedule a follow-up to cover the outstanding agenda topics.

## Reflective exercise

Make a prioritized list of important topics you wish to discuss with your boss.

For each item on the list be sure to differentiate between your activity to bring about a successful outcome and your actual impact. Use facts and data to back up your perspective.

Make a list of all areas where you need help from your boss, or at least where you think you may need help in the coming weeks. Be very specific as to what action you want your boss to take and what outcome you are looking for them to achieve.

# 27
# How to ask for a pay rise

A pay rise can make a big difference to both one's professional and personal life, as well as make you feel better about how you are valued by the company. By its nature it is an intensely personal topic, and consequently it can give rise to a lot of angst and anxiety for people. A well-managed process can have a very satisfactory outcome, but the converse is also true. This chapter will give you a process to follow, enable you to prepare and hopefully give you the confidence to have a constructive discussion with your employer. Look at your request for a pay rise as a negotiation where you want all parties to feel they have got what they want from the discussions. Ultimately, it is an investment decision and should be treated as such.

In pay rise discussions, you want the company to feel that they are appropriately recognizing and rewarding a high performer and have secured your commitment for the foreseeable future. Essentially, you are asking the company to invest in you, and the company is entitled to feel that it will get a return on that investment. Additionally, you want to feel appropriately remunerated for the role you play, the value you currently add and will continue to add for the company. You want the discussion to end on a positive note.

Tip: many people believe that salary increases, and other improved compensation, should be proactively offered by companies in return for high performance. It's a common opinion that if you just work hard and well enough, you'll get more recognition. Whether or not this should be the case, the reality is most often not like this. The old adage of 'if you don't ask you don't get' is very true when it comes to salary and benefits discussions.

# Prior to pay rise discussions

In advance of any discussion, get a better understanding of the key factors that influence the likelihood of you getting a salary increase. The salary for a role is generally a function of four key factors:

1 **The business need for the role:** in some industries a role or skill set may be more highly prized than in another industry. Most companies will set a price or salary level for a particular role based upon the criticality of the role to the business's success and the market conditions. It is important to ascertain how critical your role is to the company and within the industry.

2 **The market price for the role:** usually driven by the supply and demand of individuals with the appropriate skills and competencies in the marketplace. This is a critical factor and it can change over time, so it is worth understanding the value of your role in the market and the cost/ difficulty to replace you. Many recruitment companies will have marketplace salary reports on their websites, or you can simply do an internet search on vacancies for roles similar to yours. The job adverts will give you a good idea of the salary packages on offer.

3 **The performance of the individual in the role:** this factor is highly relevant. The question is not so much how well you perform, but how well you perform relative to others in the company and externally in the market.

When you ask for a rise your boss is presented with a choice – either they grant the pay rise, or take the risk that you will leave for greener pastures, which means they will then be faced with looking for someone new to bring the same or better performance at the same or lower rate.

A boss will usually be motivated to retain a high performer, so make sure that you can clearly demonstrate that you are delivering results, not just working hard. I rarely meet people in a company who tell me that they are not working hard – so do not base your request for a salary increase on hard work; base your request on your results and the impact you make for the company.

4 **The company's ability to pay:** this is a function of the company's performance. In the end, the company's ability to pay the increase is a key determining factor in what sort of an increase you will get. If you are clearly able to illustrate how you add value, then the company should see value in retaining you. You have an advantage in this area, as replacing you will usually be expensive – the cost of hiring a new person can equate to approximately 20–30 per cent of the first year's salary, and will take time in both the recruitment process and the training of the new employee. Retaining an

existing employee is usually cheaper than hiring a new person, assuming the existing employee is a good performer.

# Preparing for the pay rise discussion

It is important to fully understand your negotiation position before you enter the pay discussions and have identified what would be of most value to you. Only you can outline your priorities for your benefits package so be sure to have a succinct prioritized list prepared before you start.

It is important to look at all aspects of your package, not just the salary. Sometimes, there may be benefits that are more valuable to you than a pay rise, such as getting more experience, increased exposure, sponsored further education, more time off or increased pension contributions. In many instances it may be cheaper for the company to enhance these peripheral benefits of your package, and these may be more beneficial to you in the long run than a salary increase.

A pay rise discussion is a subtle negotiation usually carried out over a number of meetings, possibly spanning a few weeks.

## Step 1: be prepared

Remember you are putting yourself out there, so it is important to be prepared for a robust discussion. By granting a pay increase, the company is in effect investing in you, so it is appropriate for them to vet the investment by asking tough questions.

The company will also be looking at whether the request will spark knock-on requests from other employees, so they will be thinking about the bigger picture. In addition to the advice from the previous section, review the factors that influence the perceived value of a role and your impact in the role, then decide how to build your case under each heading.

## Step 2: know how and where you add value to the organization

Have evidence of your productivity improvements over the past year – if you can't do this then your performance probably doesn't warrant an increase in pay. Always keep a record of your achievements and any process improvements you have made, and how those improvements have been of value to the company, either in revenue generation, cost reduction or customer service improvement. Think of this step as creating a business case for your request.

## Step 3: be specific in your request

Look at your entire package and work out what would be most beneficial to you. Show how you have arrived at the pay rise or package improvement request you are making, and why you think it is reasonable.

At this step you have to be prepared to sell yourself and your worth to the company. Be balanced; don't allow self-limiting beliefs to restrict you, but also be realistic. An unrealistic request may simply give the impression that you are naïve or out of touch with the market value of your role.

## Step 4: look for allies

Are there other stakeholders who value your contribution and would support you in getting a pay rise? Who is your boss most likely to listen to? If there are people who you think would support your request, decide upon how and when to involve them in the discussions. It is probably best to start the discussion with your boss but if you feel they need some reassurance from a third party then be prepared to ask that individual or stakeholder to support you.

## Step 5: make it easy for your boss

Help your boss to help you. In many cases your boss may have to get approval for the pay rise from other senior managers or directors, so provide them with the evidence to put forward a compelling case. If they will need to take a business case to others for approval, draft it for them to make it easier – most of the content will be available after you have completed step 2 in this process.

## Step 6: be prepared to be turned down

Above all, it is always important to respond professionally. Be prepared for constructive criticism, then ask for specific reasons and feedback. Solicit support from your boss to explore ways to address these reasons and set a date for when you can reopen the discussion, for example in three or six months' time.

It is OK to express your disappointment in a neutral fashion with controlled emotion, but the key thing is to remember to respond professionally. It is important not to prove the decision maker right. If you react unprofessionally, those who made the decision will conclude they were correct as you are obviously not able to handle bad news or respond professionally when you don't get your own way.

A pay rise discussion should always be a constructive conversation, whatever the outcome. It is important that you use language that is consistent with a balanced conversation; you want to avoid your boss getting the impression that they are being given an ultimatum. It is unwise to issue an ultimatum, as not only will this make you appear unprofessional, but the company may well assume that you will come back with a further ultimatum at a later date. Any business is going to be extremely unwilling to feel 'hostage' to one employee, no matter how amazing that employee is, so they may call your bluff and start to plan for your departure as soon as you give such an ultimatum.

After you have followed all of these steps, if your request has been unsuccessful – or even if multiple requests and reviews have been unsuccessful, and you have begun to feel that you are being 'strung along' – then you have a choice. Either remain with the status quo, or take it as an opportunity to prepare your CV and test the market.

## Tips, tricks and takeaways

- **Tone:** keep the tone of the conversation positive. Express why you are excited about working for the company, why you want to continue to grow and develop with the company, and how you see the company being successful in the long term.

- **Be constructive and be prepared to be creative:** a pay discussion is rarely straightforward and it is likely that you will have to look at a counterproposal, eg instead of getting a pay rise you get a bigger bonus, shares, profit share or improved commission. If the company really values you, they may offer you more than you were looking for but defer the payout to a later date, for example, share awards that vest over five years, often referred to as 'golden handcuffs'.

- **Keep your boss on side:** don't put your boss in a position where they perceive themselves to be held over a barrel. Remember your career is a marathon, not a sprint, and you certainly don't want to burn bridges along the way.

- **Get good advice:** remuneration is a sensitive topic and should be handled discreetly. Identify a trusted adviser or mentor to help you in the process. Don't be swayed by individuals bragging, either at social occasions or at the infamous water cooler.

## Reflective exercise

1 Make a list of your package priorities. It is not unusual for some of the following to be discussed during a salary and benefits discussion:

   a base salary;

   b bonus;

   c profit share;

   d commission;

   e holidays;

   f study leave or sponsored study;

   g health insurance (sometimes including salary insurance in the event of being out of work due to long-term ill health);

   h pension contributions;

   i death in service benefit;

   j stock options or equity in the company;

   k discounted share purchase schemes;

   l training, education and development;

   m a company car;

   n public travel passes;

   o discounts on company products;

   p higher travel expenses and/or class of travel;

   q sports club, gym or social club membership;

   r ability to take unpaid leave or career breaks and paid sabbaticals.

2 Do an internet search of vacancies for roles similar to yours – assess the market opportunities.

**3** Make a list of all your achievements over the last 12 months – you could categorize them as follows:

**a** initiatives successfully delivered to increase revenue;

**b** initiatives successfully delivered to reduce cost;

**c** improved efficiency or productivity;

**d** initiatives successfully delivered to improve customer experience;

**e** initiatives successfully delivered to reduce risk or enhance compliance.

The list above must include hard quantifiable benefits as well as softer benefits.

What information have you gathered that may be helpful in a salary discussion?

# 28
# Negotiation skills

Knowledge is power in a negotiation; if you lack knowledge, you may well miss significant opportunities. Unequivocally, the most important aspect of a negotiation is the preparation and planning that is done in advance. This preparation is all about increasing your knowledge, and then deciding how and when you will use that information.

You will encounter many different types of negotiation in your career. Negotiation is fundamental to some roles, such as sales and procurement, but you may also find yourself involved in negotiations as you encounter the following scenarios:

- negotiating workload with your team or boss;
- negotiating costs or services with a supplier, vendor or other third party;
- negotiating an employment contract;
- negotiating a fee or sales price (ie when someone is purchasing from you);
- negotiating flexible working hours;
- negotiating a deadline;
- negotiating a pay rise (see Chapter 27).

There are three key aspects to any negotiation: knowledge, timing and strategy.

## Knowledge

For any negotiation, you need to understand the following:

- your needs;
- the other party's needs;
- the strength of your negotiation position.

## *Your needs*

You need to know what success from a negotiation looks like. Be very clear on what it is you are hoping to achieve:

- What would be an ideal outcome?

- What would be an acceptable outcome?

- What is your bottom line? Are you prepared to walk away if you do not achieve your bottom line? Do you have a viable alternative?

Anticipate the sticking points, so that you can respond to them. Decide what you are willing to concede and what you want in return – a good principle is to never offer a concession without knowing what you want in return. To help you work this out, it is important to know the value of the concession to you and to the other party (for example, is there something relatively meaningless to you that would make a big difference to the other person? Or is there something big you are considering offering that actually wouldn't add much value to them?) It is also important to consider when to make the concession in the negotiation process – giving away too much too early means that you are likely to give away more.

Going into the negotiation you need to be able to satisfy the following:

- **Be very clear** on your needs and the rationale that underpins those needs. This should be supported by facts.

- **Be consistent** in the prioritization of your needs.

- **Be fair:** if one party leaves a negotiation feeling hard done by this may have future ramifications – be wary of a short-term 'win' that causes losses in the long term.

- **Integrity and trust:** a negotiation requires both parties to trust the other and for both parties to act with integrity – again, watch out for a short-term 'win' that leads to a longer-term loss at the cost of the relationship. For example, say you are negotiating with a vendor or supplier; it could be tempting to use confidential information about one of their competitors – or you may even give it away accidentally. This would impact your integrity in the other person's eyes: after all, you might give away some of *their* confidential information in the future.

- **Strategy:** consider your *strategic* needs as well as your immediate needs, and how these fit together. For example: how important is your goal, need or purchase to the business? (Is it a crucial product or service purchase? Is it winning the business of a critical client? Is it a project deadline that will make a difference to your company's reputation if missed? Will whatever it is impact the long-term success of the business?)

## *The other party*

Just as you have identified and thought through your own needs, it is helpful to spend time thinking through your negotiation partner's needs. Good negotiators will spend time early in the negotiation asking questions of the other party – these questions will be designed specifically to gain a better understanding of the other party's position, and to seek out areas of common ground. However, you can also try putting yourself in their shoes beforehand – try asking yourself some of these questions:

- How valuable are you to the other person? If you are a customer – what proportion of their revenue and profit do you account for (the latter being more important)? If they are your boss – are you a high performer or an average performer? If they are a peer – do they rely on you or your work, or do you rely on them and their work?

- How is your relationship – do they view you positively, or as a nuisance?

- Are there any factors that you consider low value, but they may consider to be high value?

- How might their timescales (such as financial year and annual business patterns) be affecting their needs? For a supplier – when are their quiet periods? If you can schedule your buying for a quiet period, they may give you a better deal. For a boss or peer – are there conflicting priorities due to a financial year-end or particularly stressful time? When are the annual performance reviews in relation to your request – does this matter? Is there a project deadline to consider? For a customer – do they need your service or product immediately, or can they spend time shopping around?

- Is the person you are dealing with empowered to make decisions? What are the limits of their authority?

- Are there cultural factors that you need to be aware of in the negotiation? Different attitudes and styles of negotiation, or particular cultural differences that may affect your conversation?

- What can you do to engineer it for the other person to make a concession without 'losing face'? Nobody likes to leave a negotiation feeling that they have 'lost', so how can you ensure that outcomes are a 'win–win'?

- How can you help the other person to help you? What can you do, in regard to considering their needs, to make sure they are able to see value in the negotiated outcome? If they cannot see the value or benefits for them, it will be much more difficult for them to come to an agreement with you.

Considering your negotiation partner's needs can also help you to manage any emotion and tension in the discussion; by having spent time thinking about their needs, you will be more aware of any potential moments of tension. You can plan to take breaks to allow participants to calm down (if things have become heated), and make considered decisions or reflect on discussions.

If things do start to get heated, it can also help to try to remember: it's not personal. Never take the negotiation personally – any negotiation in a business setting is a business discussion. Even when it feels very personal – like negotiating your pay or workload, or negotiating the purchase of critical supplies for your big-dream-start-up company, or negotiating flexible hours to spend time with your family – the other person in this scenario is paid to get the best deal possible for their company.

## *Strength of your negotiation position*

The answers to the questions in the previous two sections will help you determine the strength of your negotiation position. The strength of your position will help determine how you approach the negotiation.

If your position is strong, you will need to act responsibly to secure a favourable deal, but not act in a manner that exploits your strength excessively. If you drive too hard a bargain, it can lead to long-term losses, such as a supplier taking quality or safety shortcuts, or going out of business; an employee quitting; your boss seeking to replace your role; or colleagues and peers forming negative opinions of you that contribute to a poor reputation in your field. If you over-wield your strong position and take advantage, the other person will almost certainly take action to ensure that they don't get taken advantage of again – including replacing you in whatever capacity they can do so.

If your position is weak, it may be best to plan long term. You will need to develop a strategy that will lessen your reliance on the other person as much as possible. Try using the following:

- Change your specification or adjust your needs.

- Broaden your reach for another supplier, a wider network, more diverse customers, other managers or colleagues, more diverse employees.

- Identify the deal-breakers – what ties you to this person?

# Timing

Have you set the negotiation at a time that is advantageous to you? We touched on this a little when considering the other person's needs, but you don't want to schedule the negotiations at a time of year that causes you problems. For example, have you left this so late that you are running out of alternative options?

You are looking to create an environment whereby you will have viable options, so make sure that you have thoroughly vetted the options in advance of the negotiations taking place. In the event you are dealing with a monopoly supplier, you may have to get creative about using alternative products. Or if you are dealing with your ultimate boss, you may need to consider that your alternative options may mean getting a different job. These things are all affected by your timing, so make sure you plan carefully.

Set a time frame for the negotiation process and agree the closing date for the process with the other party. You need to allow enough time for both parties to think creatively and to reach a mutually beneficial solution. You should be able to track progress in terms of resolving open items – this will also help ensure that you are not being 'strung along'.

# Strategy

In a negotiation you want to enable the other party to help you reach a successful outcome, but how open should you be with information? By definition, you will have to share some information with the other party, but you should use the filter of 'usefulness' – will the information enable them to give you a better deal, or will the information help the other party see the benefits to them?

There is always a trade-off in giving information – is it more beneficial to give the other party enough information in advance to help them give you what you want, or do you provide the information at a later point in the process? Ask yourself: when is the best time to give the information? If the information is of value to the other party, it might be worth holding it back and ensuring you get something in return for it.

# Purchasing negotiations

The principles of effective negotiation can be applied across all types of relationships and goals. However, there are some additional specific tips that may help you when making a purchasing decision, or negotiating with a supplier or vendor:

- **Cost modelling:** you need to understand the cost components that make up the product or service you are buying. Remember, approximately 75 per cent of the cost is designed into the product or service you will purchase: what determines the majority of cost you will pay is the thing you need, not who supplies it. You also need to understand whether you have any requirements that will drive up the cost for the supplier, such as a unique component that differs from the specifications of their other customers, as this may cause you to lose out on the benefits of volume discounts. Be sure to ask the supplier what specifications they are using for other customers.

- **Customer flow:** Have they recently lost or gained a large customer? If they have gained a customer, you need to be wary of capacity constraints. On the other hand, they should now be able to gain economies of scale and spread their overheads over a larger volume, so reducing the unit price to you. Alternatively, if they have lost a customer, you want to make sure you don't end up paying more of their overheads and indirect expenses.

- **Information outside the negotiation:** be careful not to undermine yourself between negotiations. For many supplier relationships, there may well be annual or bi-annual negotiations; sometimes what is said between these times can have a detrimental effect on the next negotiation. For example, boasting to a supplier about profitability increases, or lavish award ceremonies and pay increases. This only serves to encourage the supplier to seek a larger price increase as they now know you can afford to pay.

# Tips, tricks and takeaways

- **Who is doing the talking?** Good negotiators ask questions and listen – if you find yourself doing all of the talking in a negotiation, it is probably a sign that things aren't going well.

- **Likeability:** people will adopt various styles in a negotiation, but if you really want something from the other party there is a better chance of you getting it if they like you. This is particularly true if you are dealing with someone who has a significant amount of power, like your boss, or a monopoly supplier.

- **Listen and clarify:** much time is wasted in negotiations when individuals misunderstand the needs of the other party. Good negotiators will ask more questions and seek to clarify their understanding of what they are hearing.

- **Unintended consequences:** driving a bargain that exploits the other person will only encourage them to take action that may add risk to you in the long term, such as cutting corners on quality, using a different business in the future or passing you over for a promotion.

- **Confidentiality:** never divulge information to a supplier about one of their competitors. It is imperative that you retain your integrity. If you divulge information about a supplier's competitor, the supplier will assume that you will divulge their information to others and as such won't trust you with critical information.

- **Document:** write down every major decision and share the notes with the other party. It is important that all critical points are fully understood by both sides, including any collateral impact that may arise as a consequence of a decision.

## Reflective exercise

Think about a negotiation point you have coming up, and fill out the grid in Table 28.1 below.

**Table 28.1** Negotiation priorities

| | |
|---|---|
| What do I want from them? (Number in priority order) | What do they want from me? (Number in priority order) |
| What are my 'deal-breaker' must-haves? | What are their deal-breakers? |

What is my best-case outcome?

What is the worst-case outcome I would accept?

Review your answers with a knowledgeable trusted confidant or dispassionate third party prior to entering the negotiation, to make sure that you have covered all options.

# 29
# How to handle an unethical request

Every individual's and every company's values are different. This can occasionally cause an issue when there is a mismatch between your values and the company you work for, or when the course of your career brings you into a situation where you feel your integrity is being tested. When people find themselves in situations they find ethically challenging, it is not uncommon to feel unable to question the situation, to feel trapped or as if they have no choice – but it is entirely appropriate to question these things. Ethics, morals and integrity are highly personal things and for many people, feeling as if they have been compromised by work is a major cause of stress and unhappiness.

There are certain external factors that may contribute to this. For example, people who may otherwise consider themselves ethical may be tempted to bend the rules or make a poor judgement call if they find themselves in the following conditions:

- There is excessive pressure to hit unrealistic performance targets.
- Ethical behaviour is not rewarded or lauded in the company.
- Other leaders do not make ethical decisions.
- A culture of secretive behaviour exists – secrecy is the cloak under which unethical behaviour thrives.

## Your course of action

Below is a suggested course of action on questions to ask or actions to take if you are presented with a situation where you feel you are at risk of being embroiled in an unethical activity.

## Examine the context

Do you have enough information to make an ethical judgement on the situation? What specific activity is violating or could possibly violate a stakeholder's interests (stakeholders include customers, employees, suppliers and shareholders)? Be very specific; identify the potential injured party and assess the activity in the context of the letter and spirit of the law. Also assess the activity in the context of what you consider to be fair and reasonable conduct.

## Get a second opinion

Discreetly try to find a third party who may be able to give you a different perspective or provide further context. This trusted confidant should be someone who has a reasonable knowledge of the context, can be impartial (so probably not a colleague, client or manager) and be able to offer you sound advice. Present the facts and ask them what they feel or how they would respond to the same dilemma or scenario in which you find yourself.

## Set up an evaluation matrix

Look at all the options available to you, and list the benefits and possible consequences of each course of action. Specifically, ask yourself: who stands to lose what and why? What is the true cause and effect?

## Look for alternative approaches to achieve the goal

Can you be creative? Is it possible to achieve the goal without compromising yourself and ultimately the company?

## Prepare to discuss your dilemma with your boss/peer

It is important not to accuse your boss or peer of being unethical (or to imply it); simply outline your concern. In other words, illustrate the risk or perceived risk as you see it and ask them for their opinion. Express your concern as a feeling – a feeling cannot be right or wrong, it is simply a statement of your wellbeing. You could say 'I feel uneasy about the proposed course of action because I see the following consequences; can you help me see the situation differently?'

## *Prepare to make a tough decision*

It may transpire that you do not reach agreement with your boss or peer. If this happens, then you have to ask yourself if this is an environment within which you want to work. Can you reconcile the clash in values and continue to work there reasonably comfortably? If you do, are you likely to have your boundaries pushed even further at another time? Is the situation morally ambiguous, unethical, or outright harmful or illegal?

If it ever gets to this point, then ultimately the decision will be yours and yours alone, so you should be prepared to seriously consider all of the factors and consequences.

### Tips, tricks and takeaways

- **Be law abiding:** never break the law.
- **Policies and codes of conduct:** most companies have published values, policies and codes of conduct that will help guide a conversation to a positive outcome. What is decided should be consistent with the company values and relevant policies.
- **Bring your boss in early:** if possible, get your boss involved early in the discussion and make sure they are fully aware of your perspective and your misgivings – your concern should be articulated clearly in writing.

### Reflective exercise

Think about a time when you have felt unsure about the ethics of a situation, or have had your integrity challenged or compromised. What happened, and what was the outcome? Did you intervene? If not, why not? If you could choose again, would you make the same choice now, or do something differently? Why?

# 30
# How to resign

No matter what the circumstances of your resignation, it is always good to try to leave a company on good terms. It is highly likely that you will come across your current work colleagues at a later stage in your career, or they will be asked about you formally or informally at some stage in the future. It may also transpire that you will want to re-join the company sometime in the future. Consequently, when you resign be considerate of both your needs and the company's needs.

## Before you resign

Develop a clear, concise rationale for your resignation. Do not have two versions, ie one that you tell colleagues and another that you tell friends – this could lead to your integrity being called into question if the discrepancy comes out later. Make sure that your reasoning is straightforward and honest.

Most people leave a company for one or more of the following reasons:

- better package;
- better career prospects or to broaden one's experience;
- better work–life balance;
- easier commute/less travel;
- to fit in with a partner/spouse's work or other family needs;
- a perceived better 'fit' between the competencies required in your new role and your skills and experience.

Be prepared for a counter offer. Your current employer may make you a counter offer to encourage you to stay – more money, a promotion or some other improvement in terms and conditions. Before you offer your resignation, ask yourself what you would do if the company makes you an offer that is better than the new company's offer. It is good to ask yourself this question in advance so that you don't allow yourself to be persuaded to agree to something that you don't want at a later stage. Be very clear on your rationale for resigning and what may influence that decision; if you are not open to persuasion by your current employer, make that point clear if you are made a counter offer.

Check your contract to see what your company's requirements are around resignations. How much notice do you have to give? Are there any competition restrictions? Are you expected to resign in writing, or in person?

# Letter of resignation

Many people are confused about whether or not they should write a formal letter of resignation. While this is not a legal requirement in the UK, resigning in writing may actually be required by your employment contract, as mentioned above. In addition, a letter (or email) is good practice – partly because it is an accepted business convention, and partly because it creates a formal record and gives greater opportunities for clarity of communication.

Once you have determined your reasoning, prepared your counter-offer response and checked your contract, stick to your reason and include it in your letter of resignation. While many contracts will only specify that you include when your last day will be in accordance with your notice period, resigning well is an opportunity to maintain good relationships and avoid burning bridges. So, express your rationale in a positive manner, pointing out the benefit of the new opportunity as opposed to criticizing your current employer. Watch out for any implied criticism.

You can also specify your plans between now and your leaving date – again, this is about making planning easier for your company and keeping a record – these things are all important if you are to leave on the best possible terms. In addition to your leaving date, you should note any holidays you still have to take and your consistency with your contractual notice period. If you are giving longer than the contractual requirement, make that point clear. Try to be considerate of your employer; you can offer to help out with the transition to your replacement. It's also good to thank your employer for your period of employment.

# The notice period

Be specific about what you will deliver during your notice period and get agreement on those deliverables.

Be prepared to leave behind high-quality handover documents that will explain the following:

- Your key objectives/commitments and the progress being made on achieving those commitments:

  o a summary of what is completed and what is still open;

  o any risks, open issues or opportunities;

  o the views or concerns of any stakeholders.

- Any latent issues – ie any issues that are not prevalent now because stakeholders know your views, but which they may raise again as soon as you leave to see if they get a different response.

- Your view of longer-term opportunities for the role or team, or the organization in general.

- A detailed review of people on your team (if applicable), indicating their performance and any mitigating circumstances. Include your view of their career potential, their strengths and development needs, and any other information that may be relevant. Arguably, it is your successor's prerogative to form their own impressions of their new team – but it can be beneficial both to your staff and to your successor to provide the option of having your input available. Your successor can then decide whether or not to see if there is a correlation between their impressions and your views.

- Clear up any open expense claims early, and don't incur any new expenses without prior approval.

- Don't enter into any new agreements on behalf of the company without prior approval.

- Make people aware of any open purchase orders or customer/supplier agreement details that will need to be managed after your departure.

- Be sensitive to those left behind; they may be disappointed you are leaving. It may prompt them to rethink their own position and, at the very least, it will introduce change that may cause them concern or open up an opportunity for them.

- Do remind people of all that was good with your current place of work.

If you are leaving to join a competitor, then some of these things may not apply. In the first instance, you must be very clear and move swiftly to resign, and in addition, you should be prepared to be escorted off the premises and not required to work out your notice period. If this happens, don't take it personally; it is simply an appropriate business practice taken by a company to protect its intellectual property. It also avoids you being inadvertently put in a compromising conflict of interest situation.

## Tips, tricks and takeaways

- **Get the timing right:** Are you due a bonus? Some companies pay an annual bonus at certain times of the year. Leaving in Q4 of the financial year may mean you miss out on a bonus. It may be worth your while delaying your resignation until after the bonus has been paid.

- **Do not burn bridges:** do not get sucked into negative conversations about your current employer. Sometimes, if people hear you are leaving they may be tempted to open up about their own concerns or likes/ dislikes. Be sure to remain professional and don't add fuel to any rumours. You never know where your career will take you, so you should work on the assumption that your current employers may well end up being potential customers, clients or important stakeholders at some stage in your future.

- **Avoid poaching:** during the notice period, do not drop hints or offer to help your soon-to-be former colleagues get a job with your new company. After you have left the company you may choose to come back and talk to former colleagues about opportunities, but don't do so during the notice period.

## Reflective exercise

Do one last piece of due diligence before resigning. Make a list of all of the positive things about your current role and company, and compare them to the package you have been offered in your new company: what specifically will you gain from the move that could not be achieved in your current company?

Make a list of all of the things you can do to lessen the impact of your departure on your current employer. Use this list to create an exit plan and a job handover to either a colleague or your successor. This may necessitate coming back to do a handover after you have left.

# 31
# How to interview (as the hiring manager)

Review the balance of skills and competencies in your team to determine what is needed in the team as a whole. Many managers focus on the skills and competencies required for the role, rather than looking at the team needs and the needs of the wider organization.

Once you have identified the key skills and competencies needed, write the job description clearly in a manner that will be compelling to potential candidates.

## Time for the interview

### Attitude, attitude, attitude!

You can teach people about your processes, products and services, but having a positive disposition is very difficult to teach. You can't teach people to want to smile or to want to be warm and welcoming. You can't teach someone to want to serve the customer in a way that will leave a positive, lasting impression on the customer, so it is imperative to hire individuals with a positive attitude, and a personality and working style that suits the role. This might mean a disposition to work collaboratively with others on the team, or on their own initiative, if appropriate – or both!

Positive attitude can be infectious in a team, but similarly a negative attitude can have a destructive impact on team morale. Your questions in the interview should focus on getting an understanding of the attitude the candidate will bring to the team. Is there evidence from their CV or in their responses to questions that they will contribute positively as opposed to always relying on direction from others?

## *Aim high*

Do not be tempted into hiring somebody on the basis of potential alone, as there is always a risk that the potential may not be fulfilled or it may take a long time before the individual reaches their potential. Your benchmark should be to hire someone that is better than you! Someone who will raise the performance of the team.

Your success as the hiring manager will be heavily dependent upon the calibre of the individual you hire. If you hire a low-performing individual, it will reflect poorly on you as the hiring manager.

## *Do not hire yourself*

As humans, we are positively disposed to individuals who share our likes/ dislikes and have similar views on life. We find it reaffirming of our own position, and as a result we are attracted to hiring mirror images of ourselves.

If you think about organizations you have either worked for or worked with there is probably a set of characteristics that are common to most of the individuals who work there. That is no accident: companies try to re-cruit people who they think will fit in with the culture of the organization, and as humans we have a habit of hiring ourselves (ie people who share our views and perspective). Over time, a cohort of like-minded individuals is recruited into the company, which can give rise to a lack of diversity of thought.

Your key objective is to hire someone who will excel in the role and bring some fresh thought and a different perspective to you and your team. You want someone who will challenge the status quo and get you and your team to think differently.

Before making a shortlist of candidates for the role undertake a gap anal-ysis, ie make a list of the skills and competencies required for the team to be successful in the future, and compare the list to the existing skills and com-petencies within the team to identify the gaps. Having identified the gaps make sure the job description highlights the need for the skills and compe-tencies that are missing so that you can attract individuals with those com-petencies. Take time to identify new perspectives or competencies that should be brought into the team to give your company a competitive advantage.

Before interviewing, complete the following:

- Look to identify your unconscious biases.
- See if you or your team have recruited to a stereotype in the past.
- Does your organization have a stereotype?

## Conduct a competency-based interview

Having established the competencies, experience and behaviours required to be successful in the role, you need to construct interview questions that will help you establish whether the candidate has what it takes to succeed in the role.

A competency-based interview will include questions phrased in the following manner.

### Competency: integrity

**1** Tell me about a situation when others had to place their trust in you. How did you know that others perceived you as trustworthy?

**2** Tell me about a time when you had access to confidential or sensitive information and you were being pressurized to reveal it. How did you deal with the people who were pressurizing you?

**3** Tell me about a time when you had to make a decision and the consideration of fairness was important. What did you do? What was the outcome?

### Competency: drive for results

**1** What results are you trying to achieve in your current role?

**2** How do you decide what to work on each day?

**3** How do you prioritize?

### Competency: goal setting

**1** How do you hold team members or peers accountable for results?

**2** Describe a time when you had to make trade-offs in the priority-setting process.

**3** Tell me about a time when you had to delegate an important assignment. How did you determine who you would delegate to? How did you set that person up for success?

---

## Tips, tricks and takeaways

- **Delegate:** look at aspects of your role that you either dislike doing or are not good at and look to see if you can recruit someone into the team who could take that type of work off your plate.

- **Get a second opinion:** get peers or colleagues with no vested interest in the role to interview the candidate. You may be under pressure to hire if your team is overloaded with work or you are afraid that you will lose funding for the role, and as a result you may be tempted to take the first good candidate that comes your way rather than waiting for the best candidate. Your colleagues will prevent you from falling into the trap of recruiting someone who 'has potential', who you think you can train up. Inform your colleagues of what you want and they can take a dispassionate view. Involving others in the interview process also brings a more diverse perspective to the process and will help minimize the impact of your unconscious bias.

- **Avoid asking trick questions:** some people advocate asking the candidate non-standard questions just to see how they react under pressure. Examples of such questions would be 'Why are manholes round?' However, there is no evidence to suggest that asking trick questions results in a better-quality hiring decision. The interview situation is, by definition, unbalanced; the candidate may already be under pressure, so there is no need to add to the pressure.

- **Keep your questions relevant to the role:** avoid asking personal questions (even in the small talk before or after the interview) about age, sexual orientation, marital status, children or religion. A question on or reference to the aforementioned topics could be construed as discrimination, and won't help you make a decision anyway.

- **Culture and values fit:** ensure that you are focusing some of your questions to elicit whether the candidate will make a positive contribution to the culture and values of the organization/team.

### Reflective exercise

Pretend you are interviewing for your own job again.

What competencies do you need in your day-to-day work, and how might you show that you have these in an interview?

What kinds of questions would you need to be asked in order to show you can do your (actual current) job?

# 32
# New employee induction

Induction within an organization, whether large or small, is an essential element in making the role a success. The induction process allows the new employee to gain valuable insight into the organization, the culture and the working environment.

For the hiring manager, there are plenty of tips to make the whole process as smooth and beneficial as possible.

## Induction: as a manager

As the hiring manager you play a key role in determining whether your new employee has a positive start in the company. Your key objective here is to set up the individual for success.

It is important to set out clear success criteria for the role over the short (0–3 months), medium (3–9 months) and long term (12–18 months). It is also important to be able to clearly explain how you will help give them the required context and knowledge to achieve these goals. The new employee must be shown how their role contributes to the success of the team/division/company.

The essential documents to be provided to all new recruits are as follows:

- A complete **job description**, which includes:
  - o company business summary;
  - o role purpose;
  - o responsibilities and accountabilities;
  - o technical skills and experience required;
  - o business skills, competencies and experience required.

- **Outline the expectations** of the individual in the role and create a matrix for visibility (you can find a template matrix in Appendix 3 on page 203):

  o Give precise responsibilities.

  o Clarify key job functions – the areas where the individual will make a significant contribution.

  o Give an overview of the culture and way of working in the company.

  o Share the expectations of the manager and any other senior staff who will be supported by this role.

  o Be very clear on decision-making authority and empowerment.

  o Clarify budgetary and management responsibilities.

  o Clarify the structure of your department and its place in the organizational hierarchy.

  o Explain the lateral lines of responsibility and liaison.

  o Determine key internal customers and suppliers with whom they will need to establish effective working relationships.

  o Clarify the measurable objectives that will be reviewed regularly (eg how the individual contributes to the overall profitability and development of the organization as a whole).

  o The measurement criteria for the individual and the department (so you can check that your performance targets are realistic and achievable).

- Identify knowledge or competency gaps and put together a **development plan** for the individual.

- List stakeholders and latent issues that may surface once a new person is brought into the role. To do this, create a **stakeholder map** showing the various relationships, needs and any comments (you can find a template in Appendix 4 on page 204).

## Tips, tricks and takeaways

- **Buddy system:** consider appointing a buddy or mentor from within the team to help with the individual's induction into the company.

- **Arrange a follow-up:** set up a time to check in with the employee to talk specifically about their induction. Remember, there should be no surprises at the end of the probation period; the employee should be regularly made aware of their progress and how well or otherwise they are doing. (Follow-ups should be at least monthly, assuming a six-month probation.) If necessary, it is critical that the individual is given time to course-correct before the end of the probation period.

## Reflective exercise

It is critical that any new employee understands how their role contributes to the overall success of the company.

Think about a role you could be hiring for, or perhaps your own role. Using paper and pen, practise drawing up a map, or a one-page matrix, to show the alignment and relationships between the individual's objectives, the team's objectives and the company's objectives.

# 33
# Succession planning

The fundamental base principle of every for-profit business is to maximize the use of its assets to sustain the creation of value for customers and shareholders. It is people who determine how much value is derived from the majority of these assets (such as the land, building, intellectual property and so on) – this means that the company's competitive advantage is wholly dependent upon the quality of the human capital (the people) within the organization.

The purpose of succession planning, then, is to protect this competitive advantage by ensuring that the business is not impacted by either the sudden loss of key personnel – if someone quits, or becomes ill, for example – or the gradual loss of collective knowledge as people retire or move on.

## What is succession planning?

Human capital by its nature is fluid, in that people can come and go unhindered from the business. Most of your assets can be copied or imitated, but your human resources are unique to your organization and are therefore a key differentiator relative to the competition. This means that succession planning is a critical discipline that needs to be undertaken regularly. The term simply means the backup plans that you put in place to ensure that when any member of your team or company leaves for any reason, they can be replaced by someone else who brings something of equal or better value to the role.

## How do I create a succession plan?

First, identify the key job roles and the key knowledge that underpin the success of your organization. For each role or piece of knowledge, analyse:

**1** What is it specifically about the role that is critical?

**2** What would happen if the individual left suddenly?

Now, for each key role, write down the name of the current incumbent along with the names of individuals who could replace them in each of the following three categories:

- **Ready in the short term (immediately):** a list of candidates who have the required competencies and experience to slot into the role relatively seamlessly, with immediate effect. The individual would in all likelihood be successful in the role, with no significant capability gaps or development needs pertaining to the role. In other words, it would be a low-risk appointment. Don't forget, it is important to check that the individuals on your list would actually want the role – there is no point in having the name of someone on a succession plan if they do not aspire to the position.

- **Ready in the medium term (1–3 years):** a list of individuals who are showing promise, are performing well in their current role, and have the aspiration and desire to take on a more senior role with additional responsibility. However, they need time to develop certain competencies and experience before they could slot seamlessly into the open role. The company should be actively supporting the individuals to develop the necessary competencies, knowledge and experience so that they can become 'ready now' candidates in the near future. The individuals should have a development plan in place to enable them to become 'ready now' candidates.

- **Ready in the long term (3–5 years):** a list of individuals, probably early in their careers, who are showing promise, are performing well in their current role, and have the aspiration and desire to take on a more senior role with additional responsibility. However, they need time to develop the required competencies and experience, and need to gain experience in other roles before they could slot seamlessly into the position in question. The company should be actively supporting the individuals to develop the necessary knowledge, skills and experience.

Succession planning can be a motivational tool for your high performers because they see you are thinking about their involvement in the company for the long term – so it's good to let people know your plans for them!

# Tips, tricks and takeaways

- **Have options:** watch out for over-reliance on a small group of key individuals – if you put the same people on the succession plan for many roles, it may indicate that you have not got sufficient breadth of talent coming through the organization.

- **Diversity and consistency:** just as your organization should reflect your customer base, your succession plan should also reflect your customer base: how diverse is the succession plan? It should also be consistent with your performance appraisals; for example, you don't want low performers on the succession plan.

- **Flight risks:** a side benefit of creating a succession plan is that it highlights the people who are capable and ready for a move – the individuals you named as 'ready in the short term'. By the nature of being in this group, these people are possibly a 'flight risk': if they do not see an internal career progression opportunity, they may well start looking externally. As these people are your high-performing, highly regarded people, you don't want to lose them, so it might well be worth letting them know your plans for them, or finding other benefits to motivate them to stay.

- **Keep a balance:** watch out for a balance of external and internal candidates. You will need to bring fresh perspectives into the team to refresh the team over time, so your succession plan should include external candidates. If you can't name potential external candidates, then you probably need to invest time and energy in strengthening your external network.

- **Key people first:** make sure you have your top talent allocated to important roles.

## Reflective exercise

Practise your succession planning skills. Think about one role – it could be your own role, or one of your team. Follow the planning process for this role:

- Note down all the people you can think of who would be ready to step into this role tomorrow.
- Note down all the people you can think of who would be ready to take on the role with a small amount of training and investment.
- Note down all the people you can think of who might be able to do the role with significant training and investment.

Reflect on these lists. Is the first list very long? If so, these people are likely to be looking for other opportunities soon. Is the first list very short/non-existent? Then you may want to consider putting some training and development in place. Are all the names on the lists currently engaged in development plans/activities? Do you know their aspirations? How could you find out?

# 34
# Breaking disappointing news to an employee

Delivering bad news is never easy. It is important to be empathetic and considerate towards the person receiving the bad news; above all, the individual should always be able to retain their dignity.

In the long run, the recipient of the bad news will respect honesty and direct, concise language. In the short term, however, a person may have an emotional reaction, so be prepared to allow them to react to what you're saying.

## How to break bad news

The steps below are not a perfect formula for breaking bad news, but a guide to how to set yourself up to ensure that the bad news is not made worse by a botched delivery.

### *Be respectful*

Your tone and demeanour have to be courteous and focused on the person receiving the news. It is important not to take an approach, such as being light-hearted, that could be interpreted negatively.

### *Be prepared*

Be thorough in your preparation; ensure that you know your facts and that you can deliver the message articulately. If necessary, practise with an appropriate third party beforehand.

## Be thoughtful

If it is likely that the individual will have an emotional response or be very disappointed, it may be appropriate to hold the meeting in a private location and at a time when the individual can leave for home immediately after the meeting, rather than having to face co-workers.

Individuals will react differently to bad news: for some the impact will be instantaneous; for others it may take longer for the true impact to resonate with them. You should plan for the individual to be on leave for the rest of the day, or week, if the news is particularly bad. If you can grant compassionate leave, and it is appropriate to do so, it might well be worth being prepared for that; you should also be aware of the increased risk of stress-induced sick leave in some instances.

## Bite the bullet

As soon as someone knows bad news is coming, it is important to get to the point quickly. Don't go into long preambles about peripheral topics or history – if someone can sense that there is bad news coming, getting distracted by side issues or misguidedly trying to 'soften' the conversation with lots of extraneous detail will only draw out the discomfort. No more than a brief introduction to give context should be necessary.

## Be concise and consistent

Where the bad news is a result of a decision you have made – such as redundancies, performance-related firings, or passing someone over for a promotion or desirable project – you need to be able to demonstrate that you have been objective and scrupulously fair in the decision-making process. Be very clear about the reasons underpinning the decision, and use the past tense to ensure there is no ambiguity over whether or not the decision has been made. This also rules out the chance of creating false hope.

For example, saying something like: "The decision has been made to downsize. There will be redundancies, and unfortunately you will be impacted' is clearer and less ambiguous than: 'We are in the process of making a decision about downsizing… there will most likely be redundancies, but we will know more at a later date.'

The former might feel harsh to say, but it means that the person affected will be able to begin to take the appropriate actions and to deal with their feelings about the news immediately, whereas the latter – while perhaps sounding softer – will prolong the uncertainty and attendant anxiety.

The importance of clarity cannot be overstated. People can deal with bad news delivered clearly much better than bad news that is shrouded in ambiguity. In fact, the uncertainty can be far more stressful and difficult to deal with than the actual bad news itself, so try to bring as much clarity as possible to the discussion.

## Own the decision

You are the person who is delivering the message, so don't hide behind HR or 'company policy'. You need to own and be accountable for the message – especially when the news is actually as a result of a decision you have made.

## Allow time for questions

This meeting cannot be rushed; allow the individual time to express their views and emotions and request more information. They may need to vent, so let them talk without challenging them. Only respond if you think a key fact has been misunderstood, otherwise just let the individual express their opinion. Remember that an opinion is neither right nor wrong, and they are entitled to their views.

## Summarize the discussion

Close the discussion by summarizing the key points and outlining next steps; it's important to provide information about what will happen next, and what support will be offered to the person over time. Be very clear, and remember to stick to the facts at this stage.

In the event of an emotional reaction, remain calm and professional, listen to the individual, make a note of the comments made, but do not engage in a debate. It is never appropriate to engage in a debate with someone who is in a highly emotional state. Remember, they may not realize how the news is affecting their behaviour, so always allow time for them to digest the information before engaging further. The caveat to this is, of course, that you should never have to tolerate abusive language or behaviour – if the meeting gets out of control in this way, you should cut it short.

## Tips, tricks and takeaways

- **Get advice:** if you are involved in a redundancy or employment termination situation, always seek relevant HR and legal advice *before* proceeding with the meeting.

- **Don't sugar-coat the message:** sugar-coating the message only makes it more difficult for the individual to digest the true significance of what they are being told and may present false hope.

- **Don't make assumptions:** don't assume the bad news will have the same effect on all people. For some people it might be devastating, but for others it may just be the catalyst they were looking for to do something different.

- **Don't personalize the situation:** do not make statements or personalize the situation to you by using statements like 'It is difficult for me to have to tell you this' or 'I know how you feel'. Keep your opinions to yourself, only offer your opinion if you are asked for it – offer to support the individual over time and especially when the time is right for them, not for you. Do try to understand what practical things you can do to help the individual.

- **Redundancy rules:** in the case of redundancy it is normal to offer outplacement services or help with preparing to start a new career outside the company.

- **Redundancy within a team:** in a redundancy situation, those employees who were not made redundant may feel guilt or have a negative reaction towards the company, so you will have to work with them to 're-recruit' them. The process may have been unsettling and have caused them to think about external options. They may have concluded that they want to jump ship rather than wait for the next round of potential redundancies.

## Reflective exercise

Think about the last time you were given bad news at work. What made the process easier? What made it harder to deal with? How were you told? Was there anything you would have handled differently, if you had been the one delivering the news?

Try asking people you know the same questions. What worked, and what didn't? How would they have preferred to hear the news?

# 35
# Decision making

When it comes to making decisions, there are many models, processes and theories about how to do this well. It is worthwhile checking what the process is in your company: organizational efficiency, motivation and morale can be greatly improved if there is a clear, well-documented decision-making process, so it is reasonable to expect that your company will have policies or helpful information in place. Whatever the specific process in your organization, most decision-making methodologies roughly conform to the stages in this chapter.

## The decision-making process

- Data creation and analysis.
- Solicit breadth of perspective.
- Engage in open-minded debate.
- Risk analysis: do your due diligence.
- Ongoing evaluation and monitoring.

### Data creation and analysis

The likelihood of a decision being well received, or achieving its desired outcome, depends largely on the quality of the data and analysis that goes into it. Usually, the data is the foundation of the decision-making process, so thoroughly examining the quality of the data is critical. The really important thing is to turn the data into knowledge and then use the knowledge to create a business insight that will deliver a sustainable competitive advantage. As you look at the data, it is important to be ruthless in segregating facts, opinions and assumptions. It's easy for people to become so attached to their opinions that they begin to see it as fact; it is not that opinions or assumptions are less valuable in the process, but for the integrity of the decision-making process to be maintained, they must be clearly identified separately from factual data.

Where you do not have sufficient data, it would be prudent to create the data by setting up a pilot or trial prior to making an irreversible decision. The outcomes of the pilot or trial can then form the basis for the long-term decision.

Be careful not to fall into the trap of seeing only what you want to see. It is not unusual for individuals to 'see' only those aspects of the data that confirm their unconscious bias or the perspective they already held. Stage three of the process (open-minded debate) should help you understand other perspectives or interpretations, which will be helpful if you are prepared to alter or modify your own opinion.

Intuition – or your 'gut feel' – is not necessarily an enemy of the process; there may be a time and a place when you will have to make a judgement call based upon your experience. The important thing is to present the rationale behind your decision, and present it honestly. Do not be tempted to dress up a gut feel decision as something that is grounded in data, as this is likely to severely undermine your credibility.

## Solicit breadth of perspective

If the decision is going to bring you into new territory, it is good to solicit perspectives from people who have tried to do something similar, or who have dealt with similar challenges in the past. You may find research in universities or industry associations that could be useful in providing you with the latest thinking on the topic, or at least help you to identify experienced subject matter experts. Similarly, even if you are an expert yourself it is always good to check that you are in touch with the latest thinking on the topic. With the pace of change in technology, you need to ensure that an apparently unrelated development won't undermine your decision: for example, the availability of free Wi-Fi may be more likely to determine the success of a coffee shop or cafe than the quality of the coffee.

## Engage in open-minded debate

Interpretation of data is not an exact science, so it is beneficial to bring people with different perspectives together to discuss the interpretation of the data. Not because any one interpretation is better or worse, but because with a variety of perspectives you are more likely to generate a more rounded, robust business insight. The purpose of the debate is to open your mind to alternative possibilities. Frequently, after doing the first step in the process, we use the data to defend or harden our own point of view, so getting other viewpoints can help ensure that you've fully thought it through.

## Risk analysis: do your due diligence

This stage could be known as the 'devil's advocate' stage. It is natural to get swept up in the enthusiasm that builds behind an idea; in fact, this is the positive momentum that is required to give you the confidence to execute the decision. However, it is important not to get blinded by the opportunity or expected positive outcome. Most important decisions will involve a trade off or an element of risk; it is important, therefore, to take the time to look thoroughly at what could go wrong. Will there be any unintended consequences? Complete a series of 'what-if' scenarios on each key assumption. The purpose of looking at what could go wrong is not to identify reasons not to take the decision or to delay the decision-making process, but to clearly identify risks so that appropriate mitigations can be put in place. Having thoroughly evaluated the risks and identified mitigations, you should then feel more confident about making the decision or taking the risk. This stage of the process is a key part of building confidence and trust in the quality of the decision.

## Ongoing evaluation and monitoring

The making of the decision is not the end of the process! It's important to nurture the progress and any actions arising from the decision itself, so that the desired outcome is achieved. It is also important to document the lessons that have been learnt: first, so that a baseline is set, from which any modifications to the decision can be made, and second, so that others can benefit from the knowledge gained during the decision-making process. The implementation of any significant decision should be accompanied by a robust plan, clearly documented milestones, clear accountabilities for all impacted stakeholders and a very clear picture of what success will look like, and how and when it will be measured. As you make progress, be prepared both to celebrate successes along the way and to modify your approach if it looks as if the outcome will not be achieved. In the worst-case scenario, you may have to cut your losses and put the whole experience down as a learning opportunity. Successful leaders know that some of their decisions will not turn out the way they envisaged, and are always prepared to cut their losses and move on rather than having resources tied up in a lost cause any longer than necessary.

## Tips, tricks and takeaways

- **Timing of a decision:** most businesses go through an annual cycle of relatively predictable reoccurring events such as half-year reporting, quarterly business reviews, annual budgeting, customer and trade events, etc. This means that the timing of a decision can be important: for example, making a decision that requires investment after the annual budget has been signed off may result in a delay until the following year. When looking at the decision-making process, it is always good to ensure that the process is managed so that it concludes in time for any business resourcing or prioritization discussions.

- **Supporters:** for any major decision, it will be important to solicit allies who will actively support your decision. Secure commitments from influential stakeholders that they will *actively* support you and the decision. Passive support may not be enough to get a decision over the line, especially if there are competing priorities.

## Reflective exercise

Think about a decision you have to make.

Make a list of the key stakeholders – who are the other decision makers, if any? Who are the prime influencers? Who will be affected by your decision?

Now make a plan – what are the factors that these people might bring to the process? How can you solicit their input? How important, relatively speaking, are each person's needs and opinions? How might you go about getting each one on board with the decision you will make?

# 36
# Starting your own business

It is estimated only 1 per cent of start-ups succeed, with most failing within the first two years. However, despite the odds, every year many people set up their own businesses. The motivation to start up your own business can vary from wanting to be your own boss or turning a hobby into a business, through to a belief that your product or service idea will only succeed if you are able to invest 100 per cent of your time in it from its inception. Whatever your reason, running your own business is not for the faint-hearted! Specifically, you will have to: be comfortable with hard work; be prepared to promote yourself and your product in a very competitive market; be comfortable with risk; be prepared for the possibility of rejection; and be able to tolerate the associated insecurity of income. In addition, you will have to be prepared to change your approach and modify your product or service offering to meet the needs of the market. Knowing how to respond to feedback is a skill you will have to develop. Having said all that, there are many positives to running your own business. You have the freedom to make your own decisions, there is no large company bureaucracy, no company politics, you work at your own pace and you can take great personal satisfaction from any successes that come your way.

## First things first

Are you ready for the challenge? Being an entrepreneur requires, among other things, a tremendous strength of character and a level of personal devotion that will impact not only your life, but the lives of your loved ones. If you support family, they will need to be on board and willing to support you in return. This might mean financial support, doing without, or being OK with you being on the road and away from home for extended periods.

Like any other big decision, it will be helpful for you to have clearly defined success criteria, and a time frame within which you will make the decision to continue or to cut your losses and return to the world of regular paid employment. It's also good to think about why you want to run your own business – being aware that running a business may well take you away from the core work you do now. If you get a lot of satisfaction from your trade – for example, being an architect – do you really want to spend less time on it, to devote your time to running a business?

## Assess yourself

Do you have what it takes? Specifically, do you have the time, passion, energy and drive to work for nothing or virtually nothing for an indeterminate period? Are you willing to bet on yourself? Do you have the appropriate skills and competencies to run a business? Typically, you will have to be very comfortable with relationship management, selling and selling your idea in particular, financial management and the ability to promote yourself. In a new business, there are no major assets and you have no track record, so anyone investing in the business or purchasing from you is placing their trust in you more than in your product or service. You must be recognized, then, as having a credible level of industry knowledge or expertise. What knowledge or insights do you have that enable you to see a gap in the market for your product or service that other people have not yet seen?

What does success look like for you in running the business? Could you achieve that same success in another way? What is the purpose of the business? Make a list of your personal success criteria for the business: when do you expect these goals to be achieved and how will you measure the success? Be very specific in defining your success criteria; have both hard and soft measures.

## Your exit plan

It may seem counterintuitive to be thinking about how you will exit the business before you start, but it is important to understand your boundaries. You may be wildly successful and receive an offer to buy your business for a price that was unimaginable at the start, or you may have to cut your losses and exit to prevent further loss. The key thing is to know your limits before you begin. The answers to these questions are particularly crucial when you have partners involved in the business; all of the partners need to know the aspirations of the other partners, and their exit triggers. It is important to know the criteria that underpin your exit plan so that you don't just drift. Your exit plan may impact investment decisions over time. Some people build businesses with a view to handing them over to the next generation; others build businesses with the specific purpose of selling the business as soon as they can make a decent return. Neither approach is good or bad, but it is important to know which one is for you.

Thoroughly assess your goals and have a plan B. For example, if you have set up the business in the hope that a family member will take it over, and then discover that they are not interested in working in the business, be ready to implement an alternative plan.

# Some preliminary key decisions

What type of business do you want? Will you be a sole trader, have a partnership or limited company, or are you going to be an independent contractor? Will you operate a franchise, be online only or utilize both online and terrestrial routes to market? These decisions impact your tax and how other businesses will work with you, so it is important to know how your potential customers will react to the option you choose.

You need to choose a business name, a product or service brand name, a logo and possibly a tag line.

Will you be able to patent any aspect of your product or service offering?

Does your product/service contain any intellectual property (IP) that is unique to you? If so, how will you protect it?

Where will you locate your business? Proximity to customers, suppliers, distributors, competitors and complementary businesses can all have a bearing on the long-term success of your business.

The questions above may seem like trivial or tedious micro details, but they can be very relevant when it comes to managing costs and getting access to government grants. Be sure to get good advice from your accountant before making the final decision.

# The product or service

You need to have robust answers to the following questions:

- How has the world survived without your product or service up to now?
- What specific customer need are you addressing?
- What will people be prepared to pay for having the need you identify addressed?
- What will people be prepared to pay for your product or service?

The answer to these last two questions may well be different, although they seem to be asking the same thing. A customer may be prepared to pay a considerable amount to have their need addressed, but may not be prepared to pay you that amount if they are uncertain that your product or service will fulfil their requirement. Also, if there is a substitute product or service that partially meets their needs they may not be prepared to pay much more, even if your product or service fully meets their needs. Finally, if your product or service is niche, it may address a specific customer need; while your competitors may not address that specific niche need, their products or services may address a suite of other needs, which may impact the customer's likelihood of purchasing a niche product in isolation.

- What will differentiate you from the competition? Will a customer be willing to pay for that differentiation – specifically how much will they be willing to pay?
- How will you protect your competitive advantage?
- How do you envisage competitors will react when you launch the product?
- How will potential customers become aware of your product or service offering?

# The research and planning

Industry research, product category research, and customer and competitor research are very important precursors to starting a business. Remember to do the research with an open mind; it is tempting for an enthusiastic entrepreneur to do their research but only see and hear the pieces of information that reinforce their enthusiasm. If necessary, it may be wise to invite a third party to act as a dispassionate 'devil's advocate' when reviewing the research data.

## Business plan

The discipline of writing a robust business plan will help you orient your thoughts and refine your value proposition. It should also open your mind to opportunities and threats that may be inherent in the industry and enable you to prepare mitigation plans where necessary. The business plan helps you turn an idea into reality – it should not be a tedious administrative exercise but rather a thought-provoking examination of your concept, and a dispassionate picture of your business and the assumptions that prevailed at the time of writing. It will never be perfect, but it will be the reference point from which you make future decisions.

A business plan fulfils many functions – fundamentally, it is the document that establishes the credibility of the business and its management with third parties, such as investors or potential customers. It is a tool that should underpin and unify all other plans in the business, such as marketing plans, finance plans, operations plans and so on. It is the document from which all other business documents should grow: all other documents in the business should be perfectly aligned with the overall business plan. If they are not, then a fragmentation of effort will occur, possibly resulting in inefficiencies and waste.

The business plan is the 'Bible' that facilitates the following:

- It **sharpens the mind** – a well-written business plan will clearly answer tough or insightful questions about the business and the direction in which the owners want to take it in the future.

- It **brings clarity of purpose** for the business's stakeholders, investors, customers, employees, banks, etc.

- It is **the basis** of all other planning documentation, eg marketing plans, finance plans, etc.

- It **establishes credibility** with third parties.

- It is a **motivational** tool for potential employees.

## Financial plan

With the financial plan, it is good to prepare for a realistic outcome. You will then create two alternative scenarios: an optimistic scenario, where the revenue is 10 per cent higher than the realistic plan, and a pessimistic scenario, where the revenue is 15 per cent below the realistic plan. The reason for creating the two additional scenarios is to prepare you for the different decisions that will have to be made with each scenario – if you make these decisions in advance when there is no pressure or emotion in the discussion, then you can refer to these plans as your starting point when the relevant scenario becomes reality.

Remember, cash flow is crucial for most new businesses. On paper, a business may look profitable, the product or service may be well received in the marketplace... but if the cash flow is not there to support the day-to-day operation of the business, then the business will grind to a halt. A shortage of cash may mean that you will have to choose between closing down, securing more investment (so reducing your share percentage) or securing a loan (possibly putting your personal assets at risk). Be very vigilant with cash flow!

The second critical aspect of the financial plan is product and service pricing – you need to have a very clear rationale for your pricing, as this will become an integral part of your value proposition. Be very clear on your routes to market, and how you will price your product or service for each market segment. You also need to be very clear on the criteria you will use if and when you want to deviate from your core pricing model. For example, will you offer discounts for volume purchases or repeat purchases? Will you have an introductory offer for new customers? Will you provide a 'freemium' service? What will you do if your competitors drop their prices? No matter what pricing strategy you choose, it must be consistent with the rest of your product offering. If you are selling a premium high-quality product, for example, but then attach a very low price, you send a mixed message to potential customers, who may well conclude that the product must be faulty as it is being offered at a cheap price.

## Marketing plan

The marketing plan will focus on the relationship between your product or service offer and the marketplace. Specifically, the following questions will have to be addressed:

- What will be the product positioning? Ultra-premium? Premium? Mid-market? Good value? Low cost?

- What is the target market? What are the demographics associated with the market segment you are targeting? Is it growing or shrinking? What market share do you hope to achieve?

- How will you make the market aware of your product or service?

- How much are you prepared to invest in marketing and advertising? How will you spend that investment to get the most impact?

- How will you find and attract customers?

- How will you sell to customers?

## Working *on* and *in* the business

Create time to work both on the business and in the business. In the early days of any start-up, you spend much time working on the business: setting up the company, establishing your brand, promoting your idea, soliciting support from third parties, networking, finding customers and myriad other mandatory tasks that you do not necessarily get paid for! This is referred to as working on the business.

Working in the business is when you are carrying out activities for which a customer is going to pay you. There is a challenge inherent in working for yourself, in that you have to split your time between working on and in the business. If you get the balance wrong, you can find yourself with a cash flow problem. When working on the business, it is important to categorize your time appropriately between generating future revenue opportunities and non-revenue-generating activities such as submitting accounts, paying bills, planning, chasing bad debt and other aspects of business administration.

Be sure to understand why it is you want to set up on your own. Running a business is very different from being in the business.

## Know the law

In business, ignorance of the law is not a defence. It is important that you understand your obligations and how you are going to comply with all relevant standards, laws, legislation, regulations and rules. Compliance with both the spirit and letter of the law is important. Your compliance is an integral part of your personal integrity and your brand integrity: it is never appropriate or worth it to take risks with your integrity.

# Taxation

It is important to ensure that you comply with all of the requirements laid down by the tax authorities in every jurisdiction in which you hope to do business. Be sure to work with your accountant so that you know the following:

- What your tax liabilities are likely to be and when you have to pay those liabilities.
- How to keep the necessary records.
- What you will do to ensure that you submit your tax return on time.
- Where to get help with your tax planning.

# You will need support

Running your own business can be massively rewarding and a lonely experience at the same time. It can be frustrating being a beginner, or a 'small fish in a big pond' – in the beginning, it is unlikely that you will have financial security and there are many risks to be mitigated. On the other hand, the highs associated with positive customer feedback, winning new business and building an income can be intoxicating. It is important to prepare yourself mentally for the highs and lows, and work out how you are going to respond in different scenarios. Where possible, engage with a mentor, coach or trusted confidant who can help you manage the situations you may face. Some of the highs and lows can be generated by people promising you business but never actually following through; or worse still, people giving you business but not paying on time or at all. Remember: business is never guaranteed until you get paid!

There are many organizations who will provide free or virtually free products and services to help new businesses get off the ground, so be sure to avail yourself of as many as you can. The more advice, help and support you receive, the better – it may help prevent you from incurring unnecessary expense and may also throw up unexpected opportunities.

In the early days, making people aware of your product or service is going to be one of your key priorities. In this regard, your network can be invaluable. Be open minded; you may well get business referrals from contacts you never imagined would be relevant. Make sure your network is not only aware of what you are doing but also aware of how they can help – make it easy for people to help you by being specific on what it is you need. Collaboration with others (including competitors) may be necessary, so keep an open mind.

## Tips, tricks and takeaways

- **Create time to try:** Will you like working on your idea over the long term? If appropriate, see if you can practise your idea in a volunteer capacity for a charity or NGO. You get to try out your approach with a group of 'customers', you will get feedback about your product or service, and you get to see if you like the activity of providing the product or service. You also get the opportunity to give back.

- **Have a customer lined up before you start:** the only true way to validate that you have a genuine business opportunity is to secure a paying customer. If possible, try to secure a customer before you resign – without poaching customers from your current employer!

- **Modify your offering:** be prepared to modify or tailor the offering to meet the needs of the customer. Customers won't necessarily come looking for your product or service; they will come looking for someone who can help them meet their need.

- **Your model:** you need to be able to explain your business with a model. Many people ask for a model or visual of the process – especially potential investors. Your model must show the following: the inputs; the process; and the outputs of the process.

- **Focus on cash flow:** sometimes highly successful businesses falter for the simple reason that the cash runs out – be sure to pay close attention to cash flow.

- **Focus on the customer:** it is critical to understand your customer. Specifically, how does your product or service enable them to be more successful? Who are the decision makers within the company? Differentiate clearly between the influencers and the decision makers.

## Reflective exercise

Practise pitching your business idea to a friend or trusted confidant.
Ask them to be extremely critical – can you answer their questions?
What flaws do they highlight? What opportunities do they see?

# PART FOUR
# Appendices

YOUR NAME MBA
Your address · +353 86 123 4567
yourname@internet.com
www.linkedin.com/in/xxxxxxx/

**Career summary:** over X years' international leadership experience in Y, W and Z, in the A, B and C industry sectors. I am passionate about customer experience and improving the brand value proposition through the provision of excellent customer service. I am very focused on personal and team development and have attained postgraduate qualifications in XXX and YY. I am a member of the management committee of my local YYY Club and regularly volunteer at BBB. (NB: include attributes highlighted in the job description of the role for which you are applying.)

## EXPERIENCE

### DATES FROM JUNE 2010 TO PRESENT DAY
### SENIOR WIDGET PRODUCTION MANAGER, CURRENT EMPLOYER

- Delivered an X% increase in sales and exceeded my target in three of the last four years through rigorous sales process discipline.
- Reduced cost of sales by Y% through the elimination of waste in the process.
- Increased customer-facing time by X% through the introduction of more efficient ways of working.
- Brought about significant customer service improvement through the introduction of innovative new ways of customer engagement.
- Improved team morale by contributing positively to help others on the team meet their targets and also helped organize evenings out with the team.
- Worked hard with colleagues and customers to introduce the new product range following the recent change in legislation.

### DATES FROM MAY 2005 TO MAY 2010
### JUNIOR WIDGET PRODUCTION MANAGER, CURRENT EMPLOYER

- Saving or making money?
- Saving time or improving efficiency?
- Making an improvement to a process or way of working? Innovative thinking?
- Example of something that had a positive *customer* impact?
- Example of improving compliance or minimizing risk?
- Example of good teamwork?
- Example of handling change?

### DATES FROM MAY 2002 TO APRIL 2005
### TRAINEE OPERATIONS MANAGER, PREVIOUS EMPLOYER A

- Saving or making money?
- Saving time or improving efficiency?
- Making an improvement to a process or way of working? Innovative thinking?
- Example of something that had a positive *customer* impact?
- Example of improving compliance or minimizing risk?
- Example of good teamwork?
- Example of handling change?

### DATES FROM MAY 1999 TO APRIL 2002
### QUALITY CONTROL OFFICER, PREVIOUS EMPLOYER B

- Saving or making money?
- Saving time or improving efficiency?
- Making an improvement to a process or way of working? Innovative thinking?
- Example of something that had a positive *customer* impact?
- Example of improving compliance or minimizing risk?
- Example of good teamwork?
- Example of handling change?

*If you have any more previous jobs, simply list them. There is no need to give more details unless they are more relevant to the role for which you are applying than your most recent roles.*

## EDUCATION

**Educational qualifications**

| | |
|---|---|
| *Graduate:* | Bachelor of Arts, X University (1999) |
| *Postgraduate:* | MBA (Hons), Y University (2000) |
| | Diploma in YYY (2:1), X University (2003) |
| | Diploma in Gardening (2:1), Y College (2005) |
| | Diploma in Hairdressing, X University (2013) |

## INTERESTS AND HOBBIES

- ✓ Active in the local sports/drama club – state the type of activity: admin, coaching, teaching, leading, etc.
- ✓ Committee member of local chamber of commerce/tidy towns committee/church.
- ✓ List any volunteering.

# Your Name

*I'm a leader with a demonstrated ability to build innovative solutions to business challenges. I have X years' corporate, entrepreneurial and NGO experience, all geared to **delivering high quality results**.*

## WORK EXPERIENCE

**Jun '17 to Present** — **Senior Widget Production Manager – Current Employer**
- Delivered an X% increase in sales and exceeded my target in three of the last four years through rigorous sales process discipline.
- Reduced cost of sales by Y% through the elimination of waste in the process.
- Increased customer-facing time by X% through the introduction of more efficient ways of working.
- Brought about significant customer service improvement through the introduction of innovative new ways of customer engagement.
- Improved team morale by contributing positively to help others on the team meet their targets and also helped organize evenings out with the team.
- Worked hard with colleagues and customers to introduce the new product range following the recent change in legislation.

**Jan '16 to Jun '17** — **Junior Widget Production Manager – Current Employer**
- Saving or making money?
- Saving time or improving efficiency?
- Making an improvement to a process or way of working? Innovative thinking?
- Example of something that had a positive *customer* impact?
- Example of improving compliance or reducing risk?
- Example of good teamwork?
- Example of handling change?

**May '12 to Jan '16** — **Trainee Operations Manager – Previous Employer**
- Saving or making money?
- Saving time or improving efficiency?
- Making an improvement to a process or way of working? Innovative thinking?
- Example of something that had a positive *customer* impact?
- Example of improving compliance or reducing risk?
- Example of good teamwork?
- Example of handling change?

**April '11 to April '12** — **Formula 1 Racing Driver – Car Company**
- Saving or making money?
- Saving time or improving efficiency?
- Making an improvement to a process or way of working? Innovative thinking?
- Example of something that had a positive *customer* impact?
- Example of improving compliance or reducing risk?
- Example of good teamwork?
- Example of handling change?

**Sep '08 to Apr '11** — **Driving Instructor – XXX Company**
- Saving or making money?
- Saving time or improving efficiency?
- Making an improvement to a process or way of working? Innovative thinking?
- Example of something that had a positive *customer* impact?
- Example of improving compliance or reducing risk?
- Example of good teamwork?
- Example of handling change?

**Other Roles**

May '05 to Sep '06   Founder and CEO, Animal Software, UK

Feb '04 to Apr '05   IT Manager, IT CompanyLtd, UK

Oct '00 to Jan '04   IT Consultant, Consultancy Company Ltd, Ireland

Jan '00 to Jul '00   Contract Designer, Pluto Inc, Australia

Sep '98 to Sep '99   Analyst, Small Consulting Co Ltd, USA

**Interests and hobbies**
- Committee member, XXX Football Club.
- Coach of the U12 Soccer team.
- Member of the church choir.
- Volunteer with XXX charity.

## EDUCATION

**MBA**
- Hons, University of YYY, USA ('08)

**New business dev**
- Postgrad Diploma, YYY Institution ('06)

**Law degree (Bcl)**
- Hon Degree, YYY College Dublin ('98)

**Certificates/courses**
- Bottle washing (UCLA)
- Carpet cleaning (VC)
- Painting (UL)
- Product design (UL)

**In progress**
- Good Course (Institution)
- Book Learning (Institution)

## PROFILE

**Industries**
- Energy, IT, Finance

**Key skills**
- Vision and initiative
- Leadership
- Clear and critical thinking
- Communications
- Ability to motivate

**Innovation methods**
- Lean start-up
- Mom Test
- Design thinking

## INTERESTS

- Sports
- Charity fundraising
- Travel
- Family time

## REFERENCES

On request

# APPENDIX 3
## Induction review matrix

Use this template to develop your own matrix against which to measure how well your new employee has been inducted into their role. I have suggested reviews at 6 and 18 months, but you may find that 3, 9 or 12 might be more appropriate or helpful for additional review points.

| Category of responsibility |
| --- |
| Activity/input required |
| 6-month success criteria/ impact |
| 18-month success criteria/ impact |
| Comments |

# APPENDIX 4

## Stakeholder map for employee inductions

Use this template to map out who the stakeholders are for your new employee and their success in their role. What will colleagues, peers, direct reports or seniors need from the new person? What will the new person need from them? What specific information might be helpful for the new person to have?

| Stakeholder | What the stakeholder will want from the new employee | What the new employee will need from the stakeholder | Comments |
| --- | --- | --- | --- |
| eg Head of Marketing | Weekly management one-to-ones Delivery of marketing objectives | Ongoing support in the role Sign-off on project milestones | eg This stakeholder will be the new employee's direct line manager. |
| | | | |

# INDEX